A Superior

A Study of the Epistle to
The Hebrews

A Superior Covenant

A Study of the Epistle to
The Hebrews

DR. JEAN NORBERT AUGUSTIN

(DMM, DD, ThD)

COPYRIGHT

ACKNOWLEDGMENTS

My thanks and gratitude go to Mr. Michael Johnson, Chief Editor of the World English Bible (WEB)

and

To Messrs. Martin Ward and David Widger, producers of The Project Gutenberg eBook of The World English Bible (WEB) from which all Scripture quotations have been taken – except otherwise stated.

Table of Contents

DEDICATION

To Lord Jesus, the author and perfecter of my faith.

To the Holy Spirit for His indefectible assistance.

EPIGRAPHS

"9:11 But Christ having come as a high priest of the coming good things, through the greater and more perfect tabernacle, not made with hands, that is to say, not of this creation, 9:12 nor yet through the blood of goats and calves, but through his own blood, entered in once for all into the Holy Place, having obtained eternal redemption." (Hebrews 9:11-12).

"9:24 For Christ hasn't entered into holy places made with hands, which are representations of the true, but into heaven itself, now to appear in the presence of God for us; 9:25 nor yet that he should offer himself often, as the high priest enters into the holy place year by year with blood not his own, 9:26 or else he must have suffered often since the foundation of the world. But now once at the end of the ages, he has been revealed to put away sin by the sacrifice of himself. (Hebrews 9:24-26)

PREFACE

The Epistle to the Hebrews is one of the most beautiful books in the whole Canon of Scripture and, to my mind, the most beautiful Epistle.

It is unique. It differs from all the other Epistles in many aspects.

To begin with, its human author is not known to us, modern-day readers.

But it would be unreasonable to think that its author was not known to those to whom it was addressed. Besides, there are certain indications in the body of the Epistle that he was known to his immediate readers.

We shall mention them when we come to them.

This so-called "anonymity" has given rise to a number of speculations regarding its authorship.

Some have ascribed its authorship to the Apostle Paul – maybe because he is the one who has written most of the Epistles in the New Testament.

Others have thought they have identified its language and style as resembling Paul's.

A third group has associated Hebrews to Apollos.[1]

---

[1] Acts 18:24-28. 1 Corinthians 1:12, 3:4.

Finally, it has been suspected that Barnabas was behind the writing of the Epistle.

But I, personally, hold to one principle: when God speaks, I listen; when He keeps silent, I respect His silence.

For me, it suffices to know that it was God-breathed to a human scribe.

Whoever wrote it was its writer. But its Author was the Holy Spirit of God.

An Epistle is a Letter. However, *Hebrews* is not written in the format of an ordinary letter. For example, it bears no salutation at the beginning. Nor does it have the ending of a common letter.

In fact, it has more the tone of a sermon written to be delivered to a Hebrew audience.

The tone of the Epistle and the language used by the author are, however, of a real beauty and purity quite in conformity with the theme being treated – the High Priesthood of Jesus.

We invite you to begin the study of this Epistle with reverence and a word of prayer and discover the real Grandeur of our Lord Jesus as well as the beauty of His role place and His role in Heaven.

CHAPTER 1

JESUS'S PRE-EMINENCE

The Letter to the Hebrews begins in a most majestic way. Right from the start, it places God and Jesus in the limelight:

1:1 God, having in the past spoken to the fathers through the prophets at many times and in various ways, 1:2 has at the end of these days spoken to us by his Son, whom he appointed heir of all things, through whom also he made the worlds."[2]

---

[2] Hebrews 1:1-2.

"1:3 His Son is the radiance of his glory, the very image of his substance, and upholding all things by the word of his power, when he had by himself made purification for our sins, sat down on the right hand of the Majesty on high; 1:4 having become so much better than the angels, as he has inherited a more excellent name than they have."[3]

1:5 For to which of the angels did he say at any time,

"You are my Son.

Today have I become your father?"[*]

and again,

"I will be to him a Father,

---

[3] Hebrews 1:3-4.

*and he will be to me a Son?"**

1:6 Again, when he brings in the firstborn into the world he says, "Let all the angels of God worship him." 1:7 Of the angels he says,

"Who makes his angels winds,

*and his servants a flame of fire."**

1:8 But of the Son he says,

"Your throne, O God, is forever and ever.

The scepter of uprightness is the scepter of your Kingdom.

1:9 You have loved righteousness, and hated iniquity;

*therefore God, your God, has anointed you with the oil of gladness above your fellows."**

1:10 And, "You, Lord, in the beginning, laid the foundation of the earth.

The heavens are the works of your hands.

1:11 They will perish, but you continue.

They all will grow old like a garment does.

1:12 As a mantle, you will roll them up,

and they will be changed;

but you are the same.

Your years will not fail."[*]

1:13 But which of the angels has he told at any time,

"Sit at my right hand,

until I make your enemies the footstool of your feet?"[*]

1:14 Aren't they all serving spirits, sent out to do service for the sake of those who will inherit salvation?

What a glorious incipit to this Epistle!

Indeed, right from the beginning, the author presents Jesus as the summum – the culmination – of God's revelation to man.

He reminds his Hebrew audience how, in the past, God spoke to their ancestors through His prophets. And God, in His longsuffering mercy, kept sending prophets, one after another, to speak to them in diverse manners. His aim was to call them to repentance and show them the way to salvation.

But, sadly, instead of heeding the prophets' messages, they despised and murdered all those godly messengers:

"Which of the prophets didn't your fathers persecute? They killed those who foretold the coming of the Righteous One, of whom you have now become betrayers and murderers."[4]

Then, in an ultimate attempt to bring them back to Him, the Almighty sent His very best "Messenger" to speak to them: His only and beloved Son, Jesus Christ! Not only did He come to call them to repentance, but also to reveal the Kingdom of Heaven to them and,

---

[4] Acts 7:52.

more importantly, to offer Himself as a Living Sacrifice for them.

In saying that the arrival of Jesus on the world stage has occurred *"at the end of these days"*, the author of the Epistle infers that there will be no other revelation. Whoever will come thereafter, claiming to be the Messiah or some messenger from God, will only be a false prophet – a mercenary!

Once the Father has sent the Best, He has no better to send!

We see, right from the start, that the author of the Epistle projects Jesus as the main Character in this Epistle. From now on, the spotlight will be focused on Him and Him alone!

Having presented Jesus as the Supreme and Ultimate Revelation of God, the author now establishes Jesus's pre-eminence – His Superiority over all other previous messengers.

That demonstration is of the utmost importance and serves a very important purpose. As the Hebrews were still hanging on to the Old Covenant and its ordinances, the author wanted to turn their attention to Jesus, the Archetype of all the Old Testament types – the culmination of God's revelation to man.

The first thing the author says about Jesus is that He is heir to the Father over all things. This is not a slight qualification: being heir to the Mighty and Eternal Creator of all the universe means that all things in Heaven, on the Earth, under the Earth, in the seas and under the seas God belong to Him!

Next, the author says that Almighty God created the worlds [plural] through Jesus. This clearly means that Jesus existed well before the world was created – that He is Deity and that He is, indeed, the Alpha and the Omega, the Beginning and the End.[5]

Pursuing his definition of Jesus, the author says that He is the radiance of His Father's glory and the very image of His substance.

In short, Jesus is the very reflection of God.

---

[5] Revelation 22:13.

That is why Jesus says:

*"17:20 Not for these only do I pray, but for those also who believe in me through their word, **17:21 that they may all be one; even as you, Father, are in me, and I in you**, that they also may be one in us; that the world may believe that you sent me."*[6]

One day, Philip, a disciple, asked Jesus to show them – the disciples - the Father. See what Jesus replied:

"He who has seen me has seen the Father. How do you say, 'Show us the Father?"[7]

Without any offense meant, if this can help us understand this supreme truth, I will translate

---

[6] John 17:20-21, emphasis added.
[7] John 14:9.

this into human terms: Jesus is, as it were, the Almighty's Alter Ego.

This is confirmed by what Jesus said: "*Have I been with you such a long time, and do you not know me, Philip? He who has seen me has seen the Father.*"[8]

This idea will be further re-stated in other terms.

Moreover, it is Jesus who upholds everything "*by the power of His Word*". In other words, if everything exists and does not fall apart, it's solely by Jesus's powerful Word.

Indeed, when we see the order in the universe, how all the planets and myriads and

---

[8] John 14:9.

myriads of stars revolve in the cosmos with more than clockwork precision, we are bound to acknowledge the Supreme Intelligence behind it all!

The author then reminds us that Jesus *"made purification for our sins"*. That is, by offering Himself as a Living Sacrifice on the Cross, He made atonement for us so that, by His Vicarious Death, we can get back to God by faith. All our sins have been washed away by Him.

Having done that, He *"sat down on the right hand of the Majesty on high"*.

Whenever I teach on that in church, I like to tell the congregation that I don't think that, once back in Heaven, Jesus just rushed to the Father's Throne and sat there!

Remember what the apostle Paul wrote: *"2:5 Have this in your mind, which was also in Christ Jesus, 2:6 who, existing in the form of God, didn't consider equality with God a thing to be grasped, 2:7 but emptied himself, taking the form of a servant, being made in the likeness of men. 2:8 And being found in human form, he humbled himself, becoming obedient to death, yes, the death of the cross. 2:9 **Therefore God also highly exalted him, and gave to him the name which is above every name**; 2:10 that at the name of Jesus every knee should bow, of those in heaven, those on earth, and those under the earth, 2:11 and that every tongue should* *confess that Jesus Christ is Lord, to the glory of God the Father.*"[9]

The above Scriptures tell us clearly that, once Jesus had humbled Himself and ascended to Heaven, *it was the Father who exalted Him*: He did not take His position at the Father's right hand to elevate Himself!

It was like a reward given to Him by the Father in recognition for His perfect obedience till the very end and for a job well done.

Have you noticed that the Bible always says that Jesus *is sitting* on the Throne at His Father's right hand?

---

[9] Philippians 2:5-11.

Why is He never *standing*?

Well, it's obvious that a throne is made to be sat on!

But why does the Bible always say that Jesus is *seated* on the Throne?

The only time He is said to be *standing* at God's right hand is during Stephen's martyrdom:

*"7:55 But he, being full of the Holy Spirit, looked up steadfastly into heaven, and saw the glory of God, and **Jesus standing** on the right hand of God, 7:56 and said, "Behold, I see the heavens opened, and **the Son of Man standing** at the right hand of God!"*[10]

---

[10] Acts 7:55, emphasis added.

Well, under the Old Covenant, the High Priest was always busy offering sacrifices in the Temple for the people. As animal blood sacrifices did not – nor could – blot sins once for all, the Priests and High Priests had to keep going to and fro. That went on year in year out.

But, Jesus, the Lamb of God[11], gave His Blood once for all! His Sacrifice has never needed to be duplicated – nor can it be!

So, having accomplished His Work on the Cross[12], He can now sit on the Throne to rest, as it were, just like the Father rested once His Work of Creation was done![13]

---

[11] John 1:29.
[12] John 19:30.
[13] Genesis 2:1-3. 2:2-4.

Why specifically at the *right* hand and not at the *left* hand of God?

When I was studying in High School, I bought a French book on "*le savoir-vivre*".[14] It was based on etiquette - the good manners, the decorum to practise in society.

Among other things, it explained the sitting arrangement at a formal dinner. The host and hostess sit at opposite sides of the table. The most eminent male guest is placed at the *right hand side* of the hostess while the most eminent female guest sits at the *right hand side* of the host.

Then the male guest second in importance takes the place on the left hand side of the

---

[14] Social ethics.

hostess and his female counterpart occupies the seat on the left hand side of the host.

And this goes on in descending order of importance – alternating between right and left - the gentlemen on the hostess's side and the ladies on the host's side.

The practical – gastronomical? – reason behind that arrangement was that the highest ranking guests help themselves first to the best portions!

Complicated?

Indeed. But that was the way the French noble society was organized.

When I was born again and began to read the Bible, whenever I saw the phrase *"Jesus seated at God's right hand*" – or something similar - I immediately made the connection: seated at the right hand of God the Father, Jesus occupies the place of honour in Heaven! Hallelujah!

Thus, we see that, right from the opening Scriptures, the author establishes Jesus's pre-eminence. Also, we see that he is not concerned with Jesus's earthly ministry but the focus of his discourse will be Jesus's elevated position in Heaven.

CHAPTER 2

JESUS'S SUPERIORITY OVER ANGELS

The author's next demonstration is to prove Jesus's superiority over angels.

In Bible days, angel worship was practised by many. That's why the apostle Paul gave the following teaching and warning to the Colossians:

"1:16 For by him [Jesus] ***all things were created, in the heavens and on the earth, things visible and things invisible, whether***

thrones or dominions or principalities or powers; all things have been created through him, and for him."[15]

"2:18 Let no one rob you of your prize by a voluntary humility and **worshipping of the angels,** *dwelling in the things which he has not seen, vainly puffed up by his fleshly mind".*[16]

Paul informs his readers that it was Jesus who created angels. In other words, angels owe their existence to Him. Hence, He is superior to them.

---

[15] Colossians 1:16, emphasis added.
[16] Colossians 2:18, emphasis added.

Then he guards his readers against worshipping angels, lest that should rob them of their salvation.

Indeed, He is now better than angels and has received a *"more excellent"*[17] (sic) name than theirs!

Grammatically speaking, it would be wrong to say "more excellent". It would be a pleonasm[18] – there being nothing better than excellent.

But, to express Jesus's Majesty and Sovereignty by comparison, the author goes

---

[17] Hebrews 8:6.
[18] The use of more words than necessary to say or imply the same idea.

beyond the confines of human language and breaks rules of grammar!

Poetic license, they call it!

Pursuing his demonstration of Jesus's superiority over angels, the author argues that the Almighty has never said to an angel: *"Today, I have begotten you. I have become a Father to you and you have become my Son."*[19]

That is not to imply that there was a point in time when Jesus *became* a Son to God: it's just that the author is expressing that in human terms.

---

[19] Hebrews 1:5.

Haven't we seen above that God created the worlds through Jesus – that all things were created by Him?

What the author means is that no angel has ever received the kind of trust Jesus received from God. The way God treats Him - the high esteem in which the Father holds Him - is unique: no angel can claim to enjoy such high esteem in the Father's heart!

To further confirm Jesus's superiority over angels, the author of *Hebrews* says that the Father gave the following express command: *"Let all the angels of God worship him."*[20]

---

[20] Hebrews 1:6.

Pushing his argumentation further still, the author says that God makes His angels winds and His servants "a flame of fire".

But, by comparison, notice the magnificence of the words He addresses to Jesus, His Son:

"Your throne, O God, is forever and ever.

The scepter of uprightness is the scepter of your Kingdom.

1:9 You have loved righteousness, and hated iniquity;

therefore God, your God, has anointed you with the oil of gladness above your fellows"![21]

---

[21] Hebrews 1:8-9.

What a glorious eulogy! Almost every single word in it has its importance.

The most important part of it, however, is at the beginning, itself – in the way the Father addresses Jesus: *"Your throne, O God!"*

Isn't it shocking that the Father calls Jesus "God"? Does this not settle the heatedly debated question about Jesus's Divinity? How can the Divinity of Jesus be questioned with such a statement like this?

Further down, we shall see this idea reinforced.

In addressing Jesus, the Almighty uses three key words: throne, scepter and kingdom – all three pertaining to Jesus. These three things speak of royalty. No wonder Jesus is called "the King of kings"![22]

Then the Father says something to Jesus which shows even more clearly that Jesus is Divine. Besides, this statement supports, to some degree, the doctrine of the Trinity:

"...therefore God, your God, has anointed you with the oil of gladness above your fellows."[23]

Here is God clearly explicitly addressing Jesus as God. In other words, we see two Persons being called "God" – the Speaker and the Addressee!

---

[22] 1 Timothy 6:15; Revelation 17:14; Revelation 19:16.
[23] Hebrews 1:9.

Going further to establish the Divinity of Jesus, the author affirms that He was behind the creation of the world: He created the earth and the heavens. With time, they will, however, grow old and obsolete. They will, therefore, disappear but He, Jesus, will live on:

"1:10 And,"You, Lord, in the beginning, laid the foundation of the earth.

The heavens are the works of your hands.

1:11 They will perish, but you continue.

They all will grow old like a garment does.

1:12 As a mantle, you will roll them up,

and they will be changed;

but you are the same.

32

Your years will not fail."[24]

The next argument that the author brings forward to prove Jesus's superiority over the angels is that the Father told Jesus things that He never said to angels. Indeed, the LORD told Him:

"*Sit at my right hand,*

until I make your enemies the footstool of your feet."[25]

As we explained above, the "right hand" is the place of honour. To sit at God's right hand is to be invested with the highest honour possible.

---

[24] Hebrews 1:11-12.
[25] Hebrews 1:13.

To conclude his argumentation of Jesus's superiority over angels, the author gives a definition of who angels are:

"they are all serving spirits, sent out to do service for the sake of those who will inherit salvation."[26]

This settles the debate. On one hand, we have Jesus as the Creator of the earth and the heavens. He has been given the place of honour at the right hand of God. The Father addresses Him as "God" and His reign will outlive the heavens and the earth.

On the other hand, we see angels as "winds" and "serving spirits sent out to do service". In other words, angels are but servants and

---

[26] Hebrews 1:14.

messengers in the service of God. We have the example of Gabriel who was sent to the Virgin Mary to announce to her that she had been chosen by God to bear His Son Jesus.[27]

Between Jesus and angels, there is absolutely no comparison!

In a much smaller proportion, we may imagine the owner and General Manager of a multi-billion business being compared to his errand boy.

Of course, far from me to be offensive and call angels "errand boys": angels are mighty spiritual Beings and serve great purposes, as can be testified in the Bible. My point lies

---

[27] Luke 1:26-38.

only in the wide discrepancy between master and servant – between Jesus and angels.

In passing, may I draw attention to the great importance believers have in the eyes of God: angels are serving spirits in God's service, sent to do service to us, the heirs to salvation:

"Aren't they all serving spirits, sent out to do service for the sake of those who will inherit salvation?"[28]

Indeed, little do we realize that we are blessed to have angels sent by God to serve us. In the natural, we may not have a servant or a maid to help us with our household. Or, if we are

---

[28] Hebrew 1:14.

lucky enough to have one, we still need to pay him or her a salary.

But angels are sent by God to help us in our needs and difficulties at absolutely no cost at all to us! It's all part of the grace the Almighty extends to us when we become His children.

It is important, at this stage, to give a word of warning and caution against the temptation to worship angels.

Indeed, important and powerful as they are, angels must at no cost be worshipped! Only God is worthy of worship: it is His exclusive prerogative!

The apostle Paul gave a severe warning about this:

"2:18 Let no one rob you of your prize by a voluntary humility and worshipping of the angels, dwelling in the things which he has not seen, vainly puffed up by his fleshly mind".[29]

During the vision he received when he was in exile on the island of Patmos, twice the apostle John bowed before the angel guiding him, but was reprimanded for that.[30]

If the author has spoken so lengthily about angels, it is to, first of all, to establish and confirm Jesus's superiority over them.

However, he is now going to mention another reason for this long discussion about angels.

_____

[29] Colossians 2:18.
[30] Revelation 19:10 and 2:7.

"2:1 *Therefore we ought to pay greater attention to the things that were heard, lest perhaps we drift away. 2:2 **For if the word spoken through angels proved steadfast, and every transgression and disobedience received a just recompense;** 2:3 how will we escape if we neglect so great a salvation-- which at the first having been spoken through the Lord, was confirmed to us by those who heard; 2:4 God also testifying with them, both by signs and wonders, by various works of power, and by gifts of the Holy Spirit, according to his own will? 2:5 **For he didn't subject the world to come, of which we speak, to angels.**"[31]*

---

[31] Hebrews 2:1-5, emphasis added.

In the Epistle to the Galatians, the apostle Paul says the following:

"3:19 *What then is the law? It was added because of transgressions, until the seed should come to whom the promise has been made.* **It was ordained through angels** *by the hand of a mediator.*"[32]

The above Scriptures mean that the Law, given to Moses on Mount Sinai, was promulgated through angels. Under the Old Covenant, it was mandatory to observe the Law – failing which, those who transgressed it paid severe penalties.

If, therefore, words ordained through angels entailed severe penalties, how much more

---

[32] Galatians 3:19, emphasis added.

important it is for us, now, to heed the words spoken by Jesus, spread by His disciples and confirmed by signs, wonders and miracles and by gifts of the Holy Spirit!

The author of the Epistle gives us a very severe warning against neglecting the great salvation that Jesus has purchased for us by means of His Blood shed on Calvary. Neglecting or despising it will bring even more drastic punishments than those inflicted upon those who transgressed the Law promulgated by angels.

So, once again, we see that Jesus is way above angels in power and in importance.

But are those the only areas in which Jesus has superiority over angels?

Not at all for the author will now mention yet another realm where Jesus ranks above angels in hierarchy.

"*2:5 For he didn't subject the world to come, of which we speak, to angels. 2:6 But one has somewhere testified, saying,*

"What is man, that you think of him?

Or the son of man, that you care for him?

2:7 You made him a little lower than the angels.

*You crowned him with glory and honor.**

2:8 You have put all things in subjection under his feet."[33]

---

[33] Hebrews 2:5-8.

It was not to angels that God put to subjection the world to come, but to Jesus! In other words, it is Jesus – not angels – who has full authority over the world.

After His Resurrection, He appeared to His disciples and told them:

"All authority has been given to me in heaven and on earth."[34]

For some time, however, God made Him, Jesus, a little *lower* than angels. But it was for a specific and noble purpose: the Father clothed Him in humanity so that He could suffer and "taste of death" to purchase our salvation.

---

[34] Matthew 28:18.

But, once He had made atonement for our sins in human garb, God raised Him up, crowned Him with honour and glory and subjected everything to Him.

That is His humiliation followed by His exaltation that the apostle Paul describes so well in the following terms:

"*2:5 Have this in your mind, which was also in Christ Jesus, 2:6 who, existing in the form of God, didn't consider equality with God a thing to be grasped, 2:7 but emptied himself, taking the form of a servant, being made in the likeness of men. 2:8 And being found in human form, he humbled himself, becoming obedient to death, yes, the death of the cross. 2:9 Therefore God also highly exalted him, and gave to him the name which is above every name; 2:10 that at the name of Jesus every knee should bow, of those in heaven, those on earth, and those under the earth, 2:11 and that every tongue should confess that Jesus Christ is Lord, to the glory of God the Father."*[35]

His exaltation is even more supremely seen in the Father's own words, prophetically revealed to the Psalmist:

"110:1 Yahweh says to my Lord, "Sit at my right hand,

until I make your enemies your footstool for your feet."[36]

---

[35] Philippians 2:5-11.
[36] Psalm 110:1

We now learn something more with regard to the reason why Jesus came to the world in human garb. And that reason tells us a lot more about the love He has for us.

He was incarnated in order to "beget" children for His Father. That is what the Apostle John confirms in the Prologue to his Gospel:

"1:12 *But as many as received him, to them* **he gave the right to become God's children**, *to those who believe in his name: 1:13 who were born not of blood, nor of the will of the flesh, nor of the will of man, but of God.*"[37]

Consequently, those who, through faith in Jesus, become children of God, become

---

[37] John 1:12-13, emphasis added.

Jesus's brothers and sisters. And He is not ashamed to openly proclaim it to the Father:

"I will declare your name to my brothers.

In the midst of the congregation I will sing your praise."[38]

He also adds the following:

"Behold, here I am with the children whom God has given me."[39]

Going further in his argumentation regarding the reason for Jesus's incarnation, the author tells us what far reaching effects it had.

Because we, God's children, are made of flesh and blood, Jesus, too, came in a body of

---

[38] Hebrews 2:12.
[39] Hebrews 2:13.

flesh and blood in order to share our lot and endure the same sufferings we do. Indeed, while in the body, He was insulted, threatened with stoning, betrayed, beaten, spat upon and mocked. He wept before Lazarus's tomb[40] and He experienced thirst while hanging on the Cross.[41]

However great Jesus's love for us was (is), it did not stop there. He became flesh[42] so that He could experience death and, by His death, conquer Death that kept us in bondage through fear.

And that, He triumphantly did when He shed His Blood on the Cross:

---

[40] John 11:35.
[41] John 19:28.
[42] John 1:14.

"Death is swallowed up in victory."*

15:55 "Death, where is your sting?

Hades, where is your victory?"[43]

Furthermore, Jesus became flesh so as to identify Himself with us and experience the same suffering as we. He was even tempted - without, however, succumbing[44] - so that He could later help us in our temptations.

The ultimate reason for His coming in the flesh, suffering and shedding His Blood on the Cross was that He could become a High Priest to make atonement for us in the Heavenly.

---

[43] 1 Corinthians 15:54-55.
[44] Matthew 4:1-11.

CHAPTER 3

JESUS'S SUPERIORITY OVER MOSES

Having established and proved Jesus's superiority over angels, the author of the Epistle will now demonstrate Jesus's supremacy over Moses.

But why Moses?

Moses is one of the greatest characters in the Old Testament and even in the entire Bible.

As a baby, he was providentially spared from extermination. Later, in his adulthood, He was called personally by God to go to Egypt and take the Israelites out of that country where they were in slavery. To achieve that, God used him to work wonders and miracles. Once they were out of Egypt, he led the Israelite hosts through the desert of the Sinai for forty years, bearing patiently their grumblings and interceding with God in their favour. The key moment came when God called him up the mountain and handed him the Ten Commandments which became the legislation governing God's people.

No wonder, therefore, the Hebrews held Moses in very high esteem – and very rightly so.

In order to give his readers an idea of Jesus's eminence, the author will now use Moses to show how much greater Jesus is.

"3:1 Therefore, holy brothers, partakers of a heavenly calling, consider the Apostle and High Priest of our confession, Jesus; 3:2 who was faithful to him who appointed him, as also was Moses in all his house."[45]

Notice the eminent terms in which the author addresses his readers: *"holy brothers, partakers of a heavenly calling"*! All that has been rendered possible thanks to Jesus's vicarious death in our favour.

He then invites us to consider — that is, to assess, to evaluate, to appraise — and marvel

---

[45] Hebrews 3:1-2.

at the worth of Jesus, "the Apostle and High Priest of our confession"!

The title "High Priest" that he ascribes to Jesus is of particular importance in this Epistle. Apart from Deity, it is, perhaps, the highest and most eminent title given to Jesus.

This theme will be developed in later sections.

In chapter 3 verse 2, the author says that, in the performance of His Ministry, Jesus proved to be as obedient as Moses to God who appointed them both for specific missions.

This far, in the matter of faithfulness, we can say that Jesus and Moses are, in a sense, on equal terms.

But this parity ends here.

Indeed, just after that, the author announces Jesus's superiority.

"3:3 For he has been counted worthy of more glory than Moses, inasmuch as he who built the house has more honor than the house. 3:4 For every house is built by someone; but he who built all things is God."[46]

To do so, he establishes an analogy with a house and its builder. A house cannot build itself: it has to have a builder without whom it has no existence. And no house is greater than the one who built it.

---

[46] Hebrews 3:3.

Similarly, Jesus, the Creator[47], is much greater than Moses, a created being. Just like the builder has greater honour than the house he builds, so does God has an infinitely greater honour for He has built everything. When we remember that Jesus is God, as we saw above, this settles the debate over the question of superiority!

But this does not stop the author in his argumentation. He puts forward yet another argument:

"3:5 Moses indeed was faithful in all his house as a servant, for a testimony of those things which were afterward to be spoken, 3:6 but Christ is faithful as a Son

---

[47] Hebrews 1:10.

over his house; whose house we are, if we hold fast our confidence and the glorying of our hope firm to the end."

While Moses was faithful as servant *in* God's House, Jesus is faithful as Son *over* His House – that is over the Body of Christ or the Church, comprising the whole community of believers.

Moses = servant   Jesus = Son

Moses = in   Jesus = over

Moses = was   Jesus = is.

This short comparative list tells a lot about the difference between Moses and Jesus.

No-one will contest the fact that there is a world of difference between servant and Son:

the servant is a paid employee; the Son is heir to the Father – thus, Boss of the servant.

While Moses had authority only in the House, Jesus has authority over all the house.

Moses *was* once servant; Jesus *is* Son forever!

A WORD OF CAUTION

If the author has gone to such length to explain the superiority of Jesus over Moses, it must be for a very good cause.

Indeed, he now has a severe word of warning to give us:

"Today if you will hear his voice,

3:8 don't harden your hearts, as in the provocation,

like as in the day of the trial in the wilderness,

3:9 where your fathers tested me by proving me,

and saw my works for forty years.

3:10 Therefore I was displeased with that generation,

and said, 'They always err in their heart,

but they didn't know my ways;'

3:11 as I swore in my wrath,

'They will not enter into my rest."[48]

---

[48] Hebrews 3:7-11.

He cautions his Hebrew readers – and us - against not paying attention to the Word of God just as their ancestors did while they were wandering in the desert of the Sinai after they had been taken out of Egypt. They paid a severe penalty for their disobedience.

Although they had seen God's hand at work in their favour during those forty years of wanderings, they disobeyed, rebelled and put His patience to the test. They went as far as carving a golden calf to provoke Him to anger.[49]

As a result, He swore they would not enter His rest.

---

[49] Exodus 32:1-23.

"3:16 For who, when they heard, rebelled? No, didn't all those who came out of Egypt by Moses? 3:17 With whom was he displeased forty years? Wasn't it with those who sinned, whose bodies fell in the wilderness? 3:18 To whom did he swear that they wouldn't enter into his rest, but to those who were disobedient? 3:19 We see that they were not able to enter in because of unbelief."[50]

The penalty they paid for their disobedience and rebellion was that they dropped dead in the desert and did not make it into Canaan, the Promised Land. Such was the fate of the generation of Israelites who had been in bondage in Egypt.

---

[50] Hebrews 3:16-19.

The author now addresses this severe warning to his Hebrew audience and, by ricochet, to us:

"3:12 Beware, brothers, lest perhaps there be in any one of you an evil heart of unbelief, in falling away from the living God; 3:13 but exhort one another day by day, so long as it is called "today;" lest any one of you be hardened by the deceitfulness of sin. 3:14 For we have become partakers of Christ, if we hold fast the beginning of our confidence firm to the end: 3:15 while it is said,

"Today if you will hear his voice, don't harden your hearts, as in the rebellion."[51]

---

[51] Hebrews 3:12-15.

He exhorts us to be careful to heed God's Word and not give way to disobedience. Hardening our hearts and rebelling against Him will entail severe consequences. Just as our forefathers failed to enter Canaan, we may also fail to enter His Eternal Rest!

Unbelievers, especially, must be very cautious. If they hear the preaching of the Gospel and the prompting of the Holy Spirit and resist Him, the consequence will be disastrous.

This is so serious that the author repeats his caution three times:

"Today if you will hear his voice,

don't harden your hearts, as in the rebellion."[52]

The subject of rest mentioned in this chapter is of vital importance. It will be further discussed in the next chapter.

---

[52] Hebrews 3:7; 3:15; 4:7.

CHAPTER 4

THE TRUE REST

As we said above, we are now going to follow the author as he develops the theme of "rest".

"4:1 Let us fear therefore, lest perhaps anyone of you should seem to have come short of a promise of entering into his rest. 4:2 For indeed we have had good news preached to us, even as they also did, but the word they heard didn't profit them, because it wasn't mixed with faith by those who heard. 4:3 For we who have believed do

enter into that rest, even as he has said, "As I swore in my wrath, they will not enter into my rest;" although the works were finished from the foundation of the world. 4:4 For he has said this somewhere about the seventh day, "God rested on the seventh day from all his works;"* 4:5 and in this place again, "They will not enter into my rest."*

The author goes back to the creation episode in *Genesis*. As we are told there, God completed His creative work in six days. On the seventh day, He rested.[53]

That is the law of first mention. It is the very first time we see the word "rest" appearing in

---

[53] Genesis 2:2-3.

the Bible. It sets a pattern that will be recurrent throughout the Bible.

It is important to note the circumstances in which this word first occurs. God created everything in six days. Then, once His work was done, He rested. Rest always follows work.

In order to perpetuate this concept, God decreed a day of rest – the Sabbath. To make it mandatory for His people, the Israelites, He included it in the Ten Commandments.[54]

Thus, the Sabbath had to be scrupulously observed by the Israelites, failing which they were put to death.

---

[54] Exodus 20:8.

That is why, during His earthly ministry, Jesus was constantly accused of breaking the Sabbath. Whenever He performed a miracle on the Sabbath, the Scribes, Pharisees and Doctors of the Law severely blamed Him.

To refute them, Jesus reminded them that He is Lord of the Sabbath![55]

He also pointed out their hypocrisy because they also broke the Sabbath to take their animals to water even if it was the Sabbath![56]

He, Jesus, "broke" the Sabbath – as they said – but to heal sick bodies and set captives free![57]

---

[55] Luke 6:5.
[56] Luke 13:15.
[57] Luke 13:16.

The author of the Epistle now warns his readers, lest they arrive too late to enter Jesus's rest. He reminds them that their fathers failed to enter Canaan – as we saw in the previous chapter – because of their lack of faith.

<u>PROTOTYPE, TYPE AND ARCHETYPE</u>

It is important, at this stage, to understand the concepts of "prototype", "type" and "archetype".

Briefly put, a "prototype" is the first sample – the first "edition" - of something that sets a pattern for other similar items to be produced.

The other similar "items" produced on the same model become "types" of the "prototype".

An "archetype" is the perfect model against which other types are measured. It is the universal embodiment of all "types".

The reason I am referring to prototypes, types and archetypes is that the rest which God observed on the seventh day was a prototype – the very first rest in the Bible.

The Sabbath – the seventh day rest – became a type of rest.

But what is the archetype of rest?

That is what the author will explain in a moment.

But, before we look at that, we have yet another example of type-archetype to consider.

It is important to know that much – if not all – of what took place under the Old Covenant has its counterpart under the New Covenant.

"10:11 Now all these things happened to them by way of example, and they were written for our admonition, on whom the ends of the ages have come."[58]

---

[58] 1 Corinthians 10:11.

That's why, speaking of the two Testaments, we say that the New is concealed in the Old and the Old is revealed in the New!

What I mean is that the Exodus story is a perfect mirror of our life.

Just as the Israelites were in bondage in Egypt, so we were enslaved to the devil in the world – the world being represented by Egypt and the devil by the Pharaoh.

Just as Moses was sent to set the Israelites free, so was Jesus sent to set us free from the bondage of Satan.[59]

---

[59] Luke 4:18-19.

Once the Israelites were set free, they crossed the Red Sea on dry land. This typifies our water baptism.

The crossing of the desert of the Sinai with all the obstacles they encountered is our Christian walk with all the trials we have to face.

As the Israelites were led by a pillar of cloud during the day and by a fiery pillar by night, so are we led by the Holy Spirit

These are just a few of the main landmarks on the journey of the Israelites mirroring our Christian walk.

But let's get to my main point.

The destination where the Israelites were headed was Canaan, the Promised Land. As long as they wandered in the desert of the Sinai, they had no rest: they had to keep walking, thirsting, hungering and feeling despondent.

It was only after forty years of wanderings that they arrived in Canaan where they could, at last, find rest. By then, Moses, himself, had grown old and had died. It was young Joshua who succeeded him and led them into Canaan.

Note well, it was not Moses who gave them rest, but Joshua.

But did he really?

Above, we mentioned a few landmarks in the Exodus episode that mirror our Christian walk. Canaan, as we have said, was their final destination.

But what is *our* Canaan?

Canaan was defined as the land of milk and honey[60] - a land of sweet things.

What is, for us, "the land of milk and honey" where we can have rest?

That is what we shall now try to understand.

"4:6 Seeing therefore it remains that some should enter therein, and they to whom the good news was before preached failed to enter in because of disobedience, 4:7 he

---

[60]Exodus 3:8, 3:17, 13:5, etc.

again defines a certain day, today, saying through David so long a time afterward (just as has been said),

"Today if you will hear his voice,

don't harden your hearts."[61]

Seeing that some have failed to enter His rest because of their disobedience, God, in His infinite mercy, has *now* appointed *a new day* to enable those who could not enter to get in.

In other words, God has opened up a new avenue – another entrance to *our* Canaan, our place of rest!

"*Today*" in the Scriptures above is an important word. It is not simply the twenty-

---

[61] Hebrews 4:7, emphasis added.

four-hour period we are living at present. It refers to the modern era – to the New Testament times, in fact.

When did that *"today"* begin?

It began the day Jesus set His foot in the synagogue of Nazareth to proclaim His Mission Statement. That day, He was given the Isaiah scroll to read from and this is what He read:

"4:18 "The Spirit of the Lord is on me,

because he has anointed me to preach good news to the poor.

He has sent me to heal the brokenhearted,

to proclaim release to the captives,

recovering of sight to the blind,

to deliver those who are crushed 4:19 and to proclaim the acceptable year of the Lord."[62]

And when He finished reading, all those present fixed their eyes on Him and He said:

"**Today,** *this Scripture has been fulfilled in your hearing.*"[63]

He was, in fact, telling His audience that He had come to accomplish what had been prophesied by the prophet Isaiah. Among other things, He had come to *"proclaim the acceptable year of the Lord"*. In other words, He had come to inaugurate a period of grace, to announce an amnesty – a period during

---

[62] Luke 4:18-19.
[63] Luke 4:20, emphasis added.

which sins can be freely forgiven through faith in Him.

The word *"today"*, as used in the Scriptures above, describes the period extending from Jesus's proclamation in the Nazarene synagogue to the present day and will last until Jesus comes to rapture His Church.[64]

We said above that it was Joshua who, after Moses's death, led the Israelites into Canaan, their place of rest. But we asked the question: "Did he really?"

There was a good reason for us asking this. Let's see what the author of the Epistle says about this:

---

[64] 1 Thessalonians 4:13-18.

*"4:8 For if Joshua had given them rest, he would not have spoken afterward of **another day**. 4:9 There remains therefore **a Sabbath rest for the people of God**. 4:10 For he who has entered into his rest has himself also rested from his works, as God did from his."*[65]

To answer the question we asked – "Did he [Joshua] really [give them rest]? – we say yes and no.

Yes, he gave them rest in the sense that, when they arrived in Canaan, their wandering ended. They could, at last, settle down in the cities they captured from the Canaanite tribes living there. Joshua, thus, gave them rest. But it was only a physical rest.

---

[65] Hebrews 4:8-10.

The Scriptures above, however, tell us that *"there remains a Sabbath rest for the people of God"* and he who enters into this rest also rests just like God rested once His work of creation was done.

What, then, can *this* special rest be?

The interesting thing with the Bible is that it explains itself!

As we said, Jesus came to inaugurate a period of grace in addition to setting captives free.

Listen to what He says in the Matthean Gospel:

*"11:28 Come to me, all you who labor and are heavily burdened, and **I will give you rest**. 11:29 Take my yoke upon you, and learn*

from me, for I am gentle and lowly in heart;
*and **you will find rest for your***
***souls.** 11:30 For my yoke is easy, and my*
burden is light."[66]

What does Jesus mean when He refers to
those *"who labor and are heavily laden"*?

This is an allusion to the Israelites who had to
strive and suffer to satisfy the requirements –
the exigencies – of the Mosaic Law.

What is that "easy yoke" and that "light
burden" Jesus invites them to take?

Are yokes ever easy? Are burdens ever light?

These are oxymorons – associations of
contradictory terms.

---

[66] Matthew 11:28-30, emphasis added.

Jesus is, in fact, using "yoke" and "burden" in the figurative sense to oppose what He offers – grace – to what the Mosaic Law demanded.

These two terms refer to the free pardon that God gives to those who put their faith in Jesus. These can, then, break free from the shackles of the Law, thus laying down their burden.

Grace is a free gift given by God. We do not have to work for it, we cannot buy it nor can we deserve it: it is freely given by virtue of what Jesus did on the Cross when He shed His Blood.

To all those who come to Jesus and confess Him as Saviour and Lord, He gives rest to their soul.

That's the rest that Joshua did not give – nor could give!

Physical rest has nothing to compare with soul rest! Rest for the soul is a lot better than mere physical rest.

There are so many ways we can obtain physical rest. We can simply quit working. We can lie in bed or in a hammock tied to filao[67] trees on a sandy beach in a tropical island as my country[68], we can dip ourselves

---

[67] Wikipedia: Casuarina equisetifolia - common names Coastal She-oak or Horsetail She-oak. Australian pine. Accessed on 14 October 2024.
[68] Mauritius, an Island Republic in the Indian Ocean.

in a jacuzzi or have an integral body massage. There are energizing drinks we can take.

But not so for soul rest! Since it has to do with our inner being – that immaterial component of our being – it cannot be obtained by material means! Only God, our Maker, can give it to us in His infinite mercy!

Lest we fail to enter into the rest that Jesus promises us because of our disobedience, he gives us the following admonition:

"4:11 Let us therefore give diligence to enter into that rest, lest anyone fall after the same example of disobedience."[69]

---

[69] Hebrews 4:11.

In the Prologue to his Gospel, the Apostle John presents Jesus as the Word who became flesh:

"1:14 The Word became flesh, and lived among us. We saw his glory, such glory as of the one and only Son of the Father, full of grace and truth".[70]

Using this metaphor, the author of *Hebrews* gives us now a powerful definition of the Word:

"4:12 For the word of God is living, and active, and sharper than any two-edged sword, and piercing even to the dividing of soul and spirit, of both joints and marrow,

---

[70] John 1:14.

and is able to discern the thoughts and intentions of the heart.

4:13 There is no creature that is hidden from his sight, but all things are naked and laid open before the eyes of him with whom we have to do."[71]

It is compared to a double-edged sword. It is powerful and penetrating. It divides soul and spirit, joints and marrow.

Nothing is hidden to Jesus. We are all transparent before Him. Being Deity, He is omniscient and sees deep inside of us. He knows us much better than we know ourselves.

---

[71] Hebrews 4:12-13.

JESUS, OUR HIGH PRIEST

Having demonstrated Jesus's superiority over angels and Moses, and having shown us how, in Him, we enter the true rest, the author of the Epistle moves a step further and raises the standard higher: he now presents Jesus as our High Priest.

"4:14 Having then a great high priest, who has passed through the heavens, Jesus, the Son of God, let us hold tightly to our confession. 4:15 For we don't have a high priest who can't be touched with the feeling

of our infirmities, but one who has been in all points tempted like we are, yet without sin." [72]

Under the Old Covenant, the High Priest held a very eminent place in the Temple Service.

He alone could enter the Holy of Holies, the Most Sacred Place in the Temple, to offer sacrifice and make atonement for the people's sins. And, even then, he could go beyond the Temple veil only once a year – on the Day of Atonement. Entering beyond the veil on any other day would mean death! Besides, before passing beyond the veil, he had to offer a sacrifice for his own sins. No

---

[72] Hebrews 4:14-15.

wonder, he was held in very high esteem by the people!

But now, we have, in Jesus, the Son of God, a much superior High Priest. Whereas the Old Testament High Priest had to offer an animal sacrifice for his own sins, Jesus knew no sin!

While the Old Testament High Priest passed beyond a veil made by the hands of man, Jesus entered the Holy of Holies by the hands of God, through the veil of His flesh and with His own Blood.

Let us, therefore, listen to Him and obey Him. He is a High Priest who perfectly understands us, our trials and our weaknesses for, while in the flesh, He endured the same sufferings and much more!

He can, therefore, have compassion and empathy for us who put our faith in Him.

The author now encourages us to come with confidence to the Throne of Grace so as to receive mercy and assistance in times of need:

"4:16 Let us therefore draw near with boldness to the throne of grace, that we may receive mercy, and may find grace for help in time of need."[73]

---

[73] Hebrews 4:16.

CHAPTER 5

JESUS'S HIGH PRIESTHOOD

Now that we have been told that we have a High Priest in the Person of Jesus, the author will establish a comparison between His High Priesthood and that of Old Testament High Priests.

"5:1 For every high priest, being taken from among men, is appointed for men in things pertaining to God, that he may offer both gifts and sacrifices for sins. 5:2 The high priest can deal gently with those who are ignorant and going astray, because he himself is also

surrounded with weakness. 5:3 Because of this, he must offer sacrifices for sins for the people, as well as for himself."[74]

First of all, he gives us the characteristics of the High Priest in the Levitical Order.

Three characteristics are mentioned above:

- He is chosen from among men to offer sacrifices to God on men's behalf.
- Because he is also human, he has his own weaknesses and can, therefore, be lenient with his fellowmen.
- Because, as a human, he is sinful, too, he has to offer sacrifices to make atonement for his own sins.

---

[74] Hebrews 5:1-3.

A High Priest is never self-appointed: he gets his calling from God.

The very first High Priest God chose was Aaron, Moses's elder brother.[75]

Aaron first accompanied Moses to Egypt to act as his mouthpiece because Moses complained about a speech problem.

When the Israelites were in the desert of the Sinai and God called Moses up the Mountain to give him the Decalogue[76], Aaron remained below to watch over the Israelite hosts.

However, when Moses tarried on the Mountain, the people rebelled and wanted to have a new god. Strangely, with the

---

[75] Exodus 29:9.
[76] The Ten Commandments.

complicity of Aaron, they made themselves a golden calf and began to worship it![77]

In spite of that, God, in His Sovereignty, appointed Aaron as High Priest. After him, it was only his male descendants who could take the post.

Thus was established the Levitical Order for Aaron came from the Tribe of Levi.

As we saw above, only God could appoint a High Priest. It was His prerogative.

Likewise, Jesus - though God in the flesh - did not just step into the position of High Priest of His own volition: He was appointed to that post by no other than The Almighty!

---

[77] Exodus 32:1-6.

"5:4 Nobody takes this honor on himself, but he is called by God, just like Aaron was. 5:5 So also Christ didn't glorify himself to be made a high priest, but it was he who said to him,

"You are my Son.

Today I have become your father."*

5:6 As he says also in another place,

"You are a priest forever,

after the order of Melchizedek."[78]

Compared to the Levitical High Priest, Jesus distinguishes Himself in the following ways:

- He is not chosen from among men.
- He is without sin.

---

[78] Hebrews 5:4-6, emphasis added.

- So He does not have to offer any sacrifice to make atonement for Himself.
- He has entered the Holy Tabernacle made by God's Hand.
- He has entered therein with His own Blood.
- His High Priesthood is forever. It is not transmissible!
- His High Priesthood is not according to the Aaronic Order, but according to the Order of Melchizedek.

We shall, at a later stage, see more about that Melchizedek.

Suffice it to say now that the above list establishes, without contest, the superiority of Jesus's High Priesthood over that of the Levitical Order.

CHAPTER 6

JESUS'S SUFFERING

During His earthly ministry, Jesus had two natures: He was fully God and fully Man.

The following Scriptures – among many other Scriptures - clearly demonstrate that. However, His humanity is, hereunder, graphically depicted.

"5:7 He, in the days of his flesh, having offered up prayers and petitions with strong crying and tears to him who was able to save

him from death, and having been heard for his godly fear, 5:8 though he was a Son, yet learned obedience by the things which he suffered. 5:9 Having been made perfect, he became to all of those who obey him the author of eternal salvation, 5:10 named by God a high priest after the order of Melchizedek".

Sensing that the ultimate moment was approaching, when He would have to endure the ordeal of the Crucifixion, Jesus began to experience a terrible anguish:

"My soul is exceedingly sorrowful, even to death."[79]

---

[79] Matthew 26:38.

He prayed and petitioned to the Father:

"He went forward a little, fell on his face, and prayed, saying, "My Father, if it is possible, let this cup pass away from me; nevertheless, not what I desire, but what you desire."[80]

The prospect of His having to drink the bitter cup full of our sins caused Him a tremendous agony. For a brief moment, His human nature made Him shy away from it. But, immediately, His Divine nature re-took control!

Fortunately so. Otherwise, we would still be in a mess today! We would have had to die in our sins!

---

[80]Matthew 26:39.

As He prayed, He cried and shed tears. His anguish must have been very great for His crying was heard! Those who heard must have been Peter, James and John whom He had taken with Him to a secluded place in the Garden of Gethsemane.[81]

The situation was so dire that He even felt fear – a godly fear, but fear, nonetheless!

Who would have thought that the One, who created the heavens and everything else, would, one day, experience fear! He who defied the highest religious leaders of His time, who cast out demons by the numbers and who confronted Satan in the desert![82]

---

[81] Matthew 26:36-46.
[82] Luke 4:1-13.

We rarely think of these "little" details when we think of the sufferings Jesus endured! But that was part of the ransom He paid for our redemption! And He did it all for the love of us!

While He was thus struggling with His humanity, He, nevertheless, remained God — being a Son, capital S. His obedience to the Father and His endurance made Him perfect. Who else, but God, is perfect?

His suffering had two glorious consequences: firstly, He, thereby, obtained an eternal salvation for those who would put their faith in Him.

Secondly, the Father appointed Him High Priest according to the Order of Melchizedek!

To use the Olympics terminology, it was like He won two gold medals – spiritually speaking.

Having lengthily established the supremacy of Jesus in various ways in the noblest of languages, the author now uses a down-to-earth language to address a severe reproach to his readers:

"5:11 About him we have many words to say, and hard to interpret, seeing you have become dull of hearing. 5:12 For when by reason of the time you ought to be teachers, you again need to have someone teach you

the rudiments of the first principles of the oracles of God. You have come to need milk, and not solid food. 5:13 For everyone who lives on milk is not experienced in the word of righteousness, for he is a baby. 5:14 But solid food is for those who are full grown, who by reason of use have their senses exercised to discern good and evil."[83]

He tells them that there are so many other things to be said about Jesus. But they are hard to understand, especially as his readers are still spiritually immature. They are still like babies in matters pertaining to the spiritual and need to be taught further so that they may grow spiritually. Like babies, they

---

[83] Hebrews 5:11-14.

are still feeding on spiritual milk. What else he has to say about Jesus demands maturity on their part.

What a change in content and in tone! After his eloquent discourse about the super-eminence of Jesus, he now uses a straightforward language to severely rebuke them.

This is, however, not the first time we see such rebuke in the Word of God.

Speaking of the coming of the Holy Spirit, Jesus, Himself, told His disciples:

"16:12 I have yet many things to tell you, but you can't bear them now. 16:13 However when he, the Spirit of truth, has come, he will guide you into all truth, for he will not speak

from himself; but whatever he hears, he will speak. He will declare to you things that are coming."[84]

What He meant was that He still had a lot to teach them with regard to the Kingdom of God. But they lacked the understanding to assimilate everything He had to tell them. However, when the Holy Spirit would come, He would be their Teacher.

The Apostle Paul also addressed a similar rebuke to the Corinthians – albeit in more severe terms:

"3:1 Brothers, I couldn't speak to you as to spiritual, but as to fleshly, as to babies in Christ. 3:2 I fed you with milk, not with meat;

---

[84] John 16:12-13.

for you weren't yet ready. Indeed, not even now are you ready 3:3 for you are still fleshly. For insofar as there is jealousy, strife, and factions among you, aren't you fleshly, and don't you walk in the ways of men?"[85]

Paul's rebuke goes much further. He accuses the Corinthian believers of being jealous and fleshly. There was strife which caused divisions among them. Some claimed to belong to Paul, some to Apollos, some to Peter and some to Christ.[86]

They were carnal and worldly.

---

[85] 1 Corinthians 3:1-3.
[86] 1 Corinthians 1:12.

In such circumstances, Paul could not give them solid food, but fed them only on milk.

We must recognize that this situation still exists among modern-day Christians. There are still believers who still need to grow in spite of the fact that they may have been converted years ago!

That is why the resurrected Jesus has given to the Church Apostles, Prophets, Evangelists, Pastors and Teachers

"... *4:12 for the perfecting of the saints, to the work of serving, to the building up of the body of Christ; 4:13 until we all attain to the unity of the faith, and of the knowledge of the Son of God, to a full grown man, to the measure of the stature of the fullness of*

Christ; 4:14 that we may no longer be children, tossed back and forth and carried about with every wind of doctrine, by the trickery of men, in craftiness, after the wiles of error..."[87]

---

[87] Ephesians 4:12-14.

CHAPTER 7

EXHORTATION TO MOVE FORWARD

Having blamed the Hebrew believers for their spiritual immaturity, the author now encourages them to move forward in their Christian walk:

"6:1 Therefore leaving the doctrine of the first principles of Christ, let us press on to perfection--not laying again a foundation of repentance from dead works, of faith toward God, 6:2 of the teaching of baptisms, of laying on of hands, of resurrection of the

dead, and of eternal judgment. 6:3 This will we do, if God permits."

The principles mentioned in the Scriptures above have been called "the doctrine of Christ".

The author mentions six items:

- Repentance from dead works
- Faith toward God
- Teaching of baptisms
- Laying on of hands
- Resurrection of the dead
- Eternal judgment.

These six items are considered to be the basics of Christianity. They are the foundation upon which higher grade teaching must be built.

The author encourages his readers to leave those behind and move to higher grounds. God willing, that is what they will do.

Notice that the author is not merely giving instructions to his audience. He includes himself in the lot to better motivate them: "Let *us* …"

Jesus and the Apostles prophesied that, before the end, there would be a phenomenon called apostasy[88].

Apostasy is the abandonment or the renunciation of beliefs once upheld. Those who fall into apostasy are apostates.

---

[88] Luke 8:13; 1Timothy 4: 1; Peter 2:20-22; 2 Peter 3:17.

The writer now speaks about the condition of those who fall away from the faith:

"*6:4 For concerning those who were once enlightened and tasted of the heavenly gift, and were made partakers of the Holy Spirit, 6:5 and tasted the good word of God, and the powers of the age to come, 6:6 and then fell away, it is impossible to renew them again to repentance; seeing they crucify the Son of God for themselves again, and put him to open shame. 6:7 For the land which has drunk the rain that comes often on it, and brings forth a crop suitable for them for whose sake it is also tilled, receives blessing from God; 6:8 but if it bears thorns and thistles, it is rejected and near being cursed, whose end is to be burned.*"[89]

He explains the dangerous situation in which put themselves those who once tasted of the goodness of God, who were enlightened by His Word, who partook of His Holy Spirit and who were introduced to the mystery of the future world.

For him, it is impossible for such people to come to repentance again: it's as if they were crucifying Christ again!

He compares them to a land that has been blessed by rain sent down from heaven. If it produces good fruit and good crop, it receives a blessing from God. But, if it produces

---

[89] Hebrews 6:4-8.

weeds, thorns and thistles, it is rejected, cursed and burnt.

As we see, the author's words against apostates are very hard!

Far from me to contradict the author, but allow me to refer to the Parable of the Prodigal Son.[90]

The son left his wealthy father's house in the country with his share of the inheritance. Once in the city, he squandered all his money with friends and prostitutes, living a life of debauchery.

He went so far down that he eventually became a swine-keeper. He was so famished

---

[90] Luke 15:11-32.

that he craved the pigs' food, but had no-one to give it to him.

Finally, he resolved to return to his father's house to ask for his forgiveness.

Meanwhile, his father had been longing to see his son back home.

When he saw his "lost" son in the distance, he ran up to him, hugged him and gave orders that a feast be organized in his honour.

This very touching story speaks of a father's love for his son – the love of God for the repentant sinner.

We also have the repentant murderer crucified beside Jesus. Hanging on a cross, he asked Jesus to remember him when He would enter into His Kingdom. Full of mercy, Jesus turned to him and told him:

"I tell you, today you will be with me in Paradise."[91]

What the author of the Epistle is saying must concern very severe cases where the "apostate" goes so far as completely rejecting Jesus, blaspheming God's Holy Spirit and seeking salvation somewhere else.

This is my personal opinion, based on my understanding of the Scriptures, and should not be taken for an absolute truth and doctrine.

---

[91] Luke 23:43.

Quite surprisingly, after such severe reprimands, the writer reverts to encouraging his readers.

"6:9 But, beloved, we are persuaded of better things for you, and things that accompany salvation, even though we speak like this. 6:10 For God is not unrighteous, so as to forget your work and the labor of love which you showed toward his name, in that you served the saints, and still do serve them. 6:11 We desire that each one of you may show the same diligence to the fullness of hope even to the end, 6:12 that you won't be sluggish, but imitators of those who

through faith and patience inherited the promises."[92]

He is, however, confident that there are better things for them – that salvation for them is still available and achievable. It's all thanks to God who is righteous. He is not oblivious of their work nor of their love for His saints.

He wishes that they all have the same perseverance, working as diligently, being full of hope. He wishes that they imitate those who have gone on before and have obtained their promise.

---

[92] Hebrews 6:9-12.

He refers to Abraham as one who had received a promise from God – a promise reinforced by an oath.

Indeed, God promised to bless Abraham and to multiply him.

The promise, as we know, was to the effect that Abraham and his wife Sarah – they were, then, called Abram and Sarai – would have a son although they were both very old and Sarah was barren.

Abraham held on to God's promise and, in due time, they got a son whom they called Isaac. Through him, came all the nation of Israel.

Well, beyond that promise, Abraham has now received his reward in Heaven.

The reason for the author's mentioning Abraham was to encourage his readers to imitate him so as to receive their reward likewise, in turn.

THE PRINCIPLE OF SWEARING

The author now explains the principle governing an oath.

"6:16 For men indeed swear by a greater one, and in every dispute of theirs the oath is final for confirmation. 6:17 In this way God, being determined to show more abundantly to the heirs of the promise the immutability of his counsel, interposed with an

oath; 6:18 that by two immutable things, in which it is impossible for God to lie, we may have a strong encouragement, who have fled for refuge to take hold of the hope set before us."[93]

Whenever there is a dispute, to settle it, the parties concerned take an oath. But they must swear, invoking a higher power so that the oath can be binding and effective.

But, when God made that promise to Abraham, there was no superior power in which He could take the oath.

Consequently, He had to swear in His own Name – the Name above all other names!

---

[93] Hebrews 6:16-18.

His promise to Abraham was, thus, doubly buckled – by His Word and by His oath in His Name! These are two things in which it is absolutely impossible for God to lie.

His promise was, thus, immutable and irrevocable!

Abraham's example should, therefore, be an encouragement for the Hebrews to avoid falling into apostasy and cling to God's promise of salvation.

"6:19 This hope we have as an anchor of the soul, a hope both sure and steadfast and entering into that which is within the veil; 6:20 where as a forerunner Jesus

entered for us, having become a high priest forever after the order of Melchizedek."[94]

In the above Scriptures, the author likens the hope we have in Jesus to an anchor.

An anchor is that heavy piece of metal tied to a rope or a chain to steady a ship when it is thrown into the sea. It immobilizes the vessel, steadies it and prevents it from drifting.

Our hope in Christ is like an anchor of the soul. It steadies the soul and prevents it from going astray. In other words, it ensures our safe entry beyond the veil, in the Holy of Holies where Jesus, our High Priest

---

[94] Hebrews 6:19-20.

according to the Order of Melchizedek, has entered as our Forerunner!

Thus, after having addressed very stern words to his readers, the author concludes this chapter on a very positive note. He gives them the assurance that, if they hold on to the hope they have in Jesus, their High Priest, they will, eventually, receive their reward.

CHAPTER 8

THE MYSTERIOUS MELCHIZEDEK

The author has made allusions to Melchizedek on several occasions, especially in relation to Jesus's High Priesthood. He has told us that Jesus has now been made a High Priest according to the Order of Melchizedek.

But who was that Melchizedek?

To discover who that Personage was, we must go to *Genesis*, the Book of origins. This is where we shall see the very first mention of that Man.

Abram had a nephew called Lot. When God ordered Abram to leave his country and move to another land that He would give him and his descendants, Lot went with him.

However, as they both had large flocks of animals, they could not stay together because their flocks intermingled. While Abram settled near the oaks of Mamre, Lot chose to settle in Sodom.

One day, however, two large armies – five kings on one side and four kings on the other – waged a war. Lot was captured and his goods plundered.

A survivor ran to Abram to inform him that his nephew had been made captive. Abram assembled a number of men and went to set him free. The enterprise was a success: Lot was rescued and his goods were recovered.

It was then that a strange scene took place:

"14:17 The king of Sodom went out to meet him, after his return from the slaughter of Chedorlaomer and the kings who were with him, at the valley of Shaveh (that is, the King's Valley). 14:18 Melchizedek king of Salem brought out bread and wine: and he was priest of God Most High. 14:19 He blessed him, and said, "Blessed be Abram of God Most High, possessor of heaven and earth: 14:20 and blessed be God Most High,

who has delivered your enemies into your hand.

Abram gave him a tenth of all."[95]

Chedorlaomer, king of Elam, went out to meet Abram in the valley of Shaveh.

Mysteriously, Melchizedek also appeared. He brought with him wine and bread!

Who was that Man?

He was king of Salem and priest of the Most High God. What an eminent title!

He blessed Abram in the Name of God Almighty and blessed God, too, for He had given victory to Abram.

---

[95] Genesis 14:17-20.

In return, Abram gave him "a tenth of everything".

You talk of a meeting!

Let us see a few things about this meeting.

First of all, no previous mention had been made of Melchizedek: that was the very first time he appeared on the world scene!

Who was that Man? Where did He come from? Who were his relatives?

Nothing is said about him!

Secondly, he was not at all involved in the battle like Abram and Chedorlaomer had been. Who, then, convened him to that meeting? How did he know Abram and Chedorlaomer were meeting there?

Thirdly, why did he bring wine and bread –
of all the other "foods" he could have
brought?

Fourthly, he blessed Abram, the patriarch
(we shall later see that there is a "clue" in this
act).

Fifthly, he blessed God Almighty, too (a
further "clue"!).

Sixthly, Abram gave him "a tenth of
everything".

Does this scene not remind us of a Sunday
Service in church?

There was a Priest – Melchizedek.

There were wine and bread – the two
elements symbolizing the Blood and the

Body of Jesus, used for the Holy Communion. It would not be illogical to say that they partook of those.

There was worship – Melchizedek blessed God Almighty.

Abram gave to Melchizedek "a tenth of everything" – they collected tithes!

What could be that "tenth of everything"?

Today, we pay tithes in whatever currency we use. In those days, however, they had no money as we do now.

It was customary, in those days, for a victorious king to take back with him a booty – whatever valuables he could take from the vanquished enemy.

A booty could also be in terms of human captives.

The "tenth of everything" that Abram gave to Melchizedek must have been taken from his booty.

Already we see that that Melchizedek was no ordinary person. To have appeared from nowhere, to have brought bread and wine, to have blessed the great Abram, to have blessed ... God Almighty and to have received tithes from Abram, he must, indeed, have been a most extraordinary Personage!

However "nebulous" he is, as we have seen, there is more to the mystery enveloping this Personage, as we shall see:

"7:1 For this Melchizedek, king of Salem, priest of God Most High, who met Abraham returning from the slaughter of the kings and blessed him, 7:2 to whom also Abraham divided a tenth part of all (being first, by interpretation, king of righteousness, and then also king of Salem, which is king of peace; 7:3 without father, without mother, without genealogy, having neither beginning of days nor end of life, but made like the Son of God), remains a priest continually. 7:4 Now consider how great this man was, to whom even Abraham, the patriarch, gave a tenth out of the best spoils."[96]

---

[96] Hebrews 7:1-4.

In addition to what we know of him already, we now learn that he is also king of Salem (Jerusalem), king of righteousness and king of peace.

More bizarrely, he is without father, without mother and without genealogy. He has no beginning of days and no end of life. He is made like the son of God and he remains Priest forever!

What a unique and glorious C.V![97]

---

[97] Curriculum Vitae: a brief account of a person's education, qualifications, and previous occupations, typically sent with a job application. (Google definition).

Here is a Man who has no father, no mother and no genealogy. The Man from nowhere, why!

He is king of Salem, king of righteousness and King of peace: doesn't that remind us of Jesus who is the Prince of Peace?[98]

He has no beginning of days[99] and no end of life. And Jesus is the Alpha and the Omega, the Beginning and the End.[100]

He is made like the Son of God. In case there was any doubt about Melchizedek's identity, this settles the matter for good: Jesus is the Son of God![101]

---

[98] Isaiah 9:6; Romans 16:20; Philippians 4:9.
[99] John 1: Hebrews 5:5,
[100] Revelation 1:8, Revelation 21:6; 22:13.
[101] John 3:16.

Mwelchizedek is Priest forever and so is Jesus![102]

As we have already seen, Jesus is now High Priest in Heaven for ever.

One thing is sure: there cannot be two eternal High Priests!

When I base myself on all the above, I have no doubt that Melchizedek was a Christophany – an apparition of the pre-incarnate Jesus. It is, indeed, hard to find another Personage whose likeness can come this close to Jesus!

Besides, there are a number of other cases where the pre-incarnate Jesus appeared to

---

[102] Hebrews 5:6.

certain Biblical characters – such as the Angel of the LORD appearing to Hagar[103] in the desert and to Gideon.[104] The Fourth Man in the fiery furnace with Daniel's three companions, Meschac, Shadrach and Abed Nego.[105]

But it is not the object of this book to delve into this subject. Enough to know that the eternal Jesus appeared on certain special occasions before His Incarnation.

When we remember that no less a person than the great patriarch Abraham paid tithes to Melchizedek, that gives us an idea of the high degree of eminence of that Melchizedek!

---

[103] Genesis 16:7-10.
[104] Judges 6:11-14.
[105] Daniel 3:25.

This is even more evident when we realize that tithes are due to God only:

"27:30 "'All the tithe of the land, whether of the seed of the land or of the fruit of the trees, is Yahweh's. It is holy to Yahweh."[106]

"27:32 All the tithe of the herds or the flocks, whatever passes under the rod, the tenth shall be holy to Yahweh."[107]

Now that we have got a clearer idea of who that Melchizedek was (is), we are in a better position to assess the full implication of the phrase *"a High Priest according to the Order of Melchizedek"* in relation to Jesus!

---

[106] Leviticus 27:30.
[107] Leviticus 27:32.

CHAPTER 9

TRANSITIONING FROM AARON TO MELCHIZEDEK

In studying the Letter to the Hebrews, we must never lose track of one idea – the very theme of the whole Epistle: the Superiority of Jesus over all else!

Having shown His superiority over Angels and Moses, the author is now going to establish the superiority of the Order of Melchizedek over the Aaronic Order and hence, the superiority of Jesus's Priesthood over that of the Old Testament Priests.

"7:5 They indeed of the sons of Levi who receive the priest's office have a commandment to take tithes of the people according to the law, that is, of their brothers, though these have come out of the body of Abraham, 7:6 but he whose genealogy is not counted from them has accepted tithes from Abraham, and has blessed him who has the promises."[108]

He begins his argumentation by referring to the question of tithes.

The priests of the Aaronic Order – those of the tribe of Levi – were obligated by the Mosaic Law to collect tithes from their own brothers. Yet, these came out of the loins of

---

Abraham who, himself, gave tithes to Melchizedek!

This gives us an idea of how great that Man Melchizedek was (is)!

If we consider Melchizedek as an *alter ego* of Jesus, by ricochet, this tells us how supremely eminent Jesus is!

In the previous chapter, when we mentioned tithes, we said there was an "clue" therein.

Tithes, as we have seen, are due to God alone. Now, the great Abraham gave tithes to Melchizedek!

Does this not prove that Melchizedek was a Divine Being – that is, the Pre-incarnate

Jesus as we demonstrated in the previous chapter?

Another proof that Melchizedek – or Jesus – is much greater than Abraham is that it is irrefutably the greater who blesses the lesser.[109] Since it was Melchizedek who blessed Abraham – and not the other way round - it goes without saying that the former is superior to the latter! In clear terms, Jesus is superior to Abraham.

In the previous chapter, in relation to the blessing of Abram by Melchizedek, we said that there was a clue there. That clue is that the Bible makes it clear that it is the Greater who blesses the Lesser.

---

[109] Hebrews 7:7.

If Melchizedek blessed Abram, the logical conclusion is that Melchizedek was (is) greater than Abram!

As no human being can claim to be greater than Abram – the Patriarch to whom God made the Promise – it goes without saying that Melchizedek was (is) a much higher Personage. That's yet another proof that Melchizedek was an apparition of the Pre-incarnate Jesus!

Another argument brought forward by the author is that, in the Aaronic Order, the Priests who receive tithes are mortal men. However, in the case of Melchizedek – Jesus

– tithes were given to the One "who has no "*neither beginning of days nor end of life*"![110]

Pushing his argument still further, the author refers to Levi. The third son of Jacob and Leah, he became the head of the tribe bearing his name. God commanded that only the males from that tribe were to be priests.

The point that the author wants to make is that even Levi, the head of all the priestly tribe, who received tithes from his compatriots, paid *his own* tithes through Abraham: when the latter paid tithes to Melchizedek, he paid tithes collectively for all the Levitical priesthood![111]

---

[110] Hebrews 7:3.
[111] Hebrews 7:9-10.

The author now raises a question:

"7:11 Now if there was perfection through the Levitical priesthood (for under it the people have received the law), what further need was there for another priest to arise after the order of Melchizedek, and not be called after the order of Aaron?"[112]

Nobody is perfect. Only God is!

He created us perfect, however, for we were created in His own image, in His own likeness.[113]

It was the first couple's sin – Adam and Eve's – that robbed us of our perfection.

---

[112] Hebrews 7:11.
[113] Genesis 1:27.

In His infinite mercy, however, God has always had one aim: restore our original glory[114], thus bring us back to a state of perfection.

The giving of the Law to Moses was part of God's Plan to bring us back to glory. But, as the Apostle Paul explains in his Letter to the Romans and more lengthily in his Letter to the Galatians, the Law was only one step in that process. Paul compares it to a school master to lead us to Christ, the embodiment of perfection.

"3:24 ... the law has become our tutor to bring us to Christ, that we might be justified by faith. 3:25 But now that faith has come, we

---

[114] Hebrews 2:10.

are no longer under a tutor. 3:26 For you are all children of God, through faith in Christ Jesus."[115]

The Law, as we see, could not bring anybody to perfection. On the contrary, it showed us our imperfection, our impossibility to fully please God.

That is why the author of *Hebrews* says:

"7:11 Now if there was perfection through the Levitical priesthood (for under it the people have received the law), what further need was there for another priest to arise after the order of Melchizedek, and not be called after the order of Aaron?"[116]

---

[115] Galatians 3:24-26.
[116] Hebrews 7:11.

His question is a most pertinent one. If, indeed, we were made perfect by the Levitical Order, there would be no need to introduce a new Order based on the High Priesthood of Melchizedek.

In so doing, God, Himself, was showing that the Old Order was inefficient and had become obsolete.

Allow me to establish an analogy with politics.

In the U.S., for example, when the Democratic Party is in power, it applies its programme to lead the country towards the vision it has set.

But, if a Republican President is elected at the next elections, the new administration applies its manifesto and gives a new direction to the country.

This is true for all countries where democratic elections are held.

Similarly, as long as the Levitical Order was in effect, the Priesthood was carried out as we have already explained. The High Priest offered a blood sacrifice for his own sins before offering sacrifices on behalf of the people. He entered the Holy of Holies only once a year, passing behind a veil made by the hands of men. After his death, the Priesthood passed on to his son or to somebody of the same tribe – that of Levi.

But, with the Ascension of Jesus to Heaven, things have changed radically:

"7:12 *For the priesthood being changed, there is of necessity a change made also in the law.* 7:13 For he of whom these things are said belongs to another tribe, from which no one has officiated at the altar. 7:14 For it is evident that our Lord has sprung out of Judah, about which tribe Moses spoke nothing concerning priesthood. 7:15 This is yet more abundantly evident, if after the likeness of Melchizedek there arises another priest, 7:16 who has been made, not after the law of a fleshly commandment, but after the power of an endless life: 7:17 for it is testified,

"You are a priest forever,

according to the order of Melchizedek."[117]

The Scriptures quoted above are very important if we want to understand the implications of the change that has occurred now that the Resurrected Jesus is seated at the Right Hand of the Father on the Throne.

There is change in the Law. To mark this change, God initiates a New Order. Whereas the Levitical Priests all came from the Tribe of Levi, Jesus, the New High Priest, originates from the Tribe of Judah. A novelty!

---

[117] Hebrews 7:12-17, emphasis added.

Moses had received no instruction from God about the Tribe of Judah regarding the Priesthood. None from the Tribe of Judah was originally authorized to exercise the Priesthood.

The change was, therefore, a revolutionary one!

Moreover, God confirms that change by declaring Jesus *"a Priest forever according to the Order of Melchizedek"*.

The High Priesthood is no longer transmissible: it's permanent!

To show its superiority, the author cites its other characteristics:

"7:26 For such a high priest was fitting for us: holy, guiltless, undefiled, separated from sinners, and made higher than the heavens; 7:27 who doesn't need, like those high priests, to offer up sacrifices daily, first for his own sins, and then for the sins of the people. For he did this once for all, when he offered up himself. 7:28 For the law appoints men as high priests who have weakness, but the word of the oath which came after the law appoints a Son forever who has been perfected."[118]

Let us list the attributes of Jesus and the characteristics of His High Priesthood:

- He is holy

---

[118] Hebrews 7:26-28.

- He is guiltless
- He is undefiled
- He is separated from sinners
- He is made higher than the heavens
- He does not have to offer sacrifices for Himself daily
- He does not have to offer any more sacrifices for the people
- The Blood He shed on the Cross was all the sacrifice that was needed
- His High Priesthood was accompanied by an oath sworn by God
- His High Priesthood is forever.

This outline suffices to prove once for all that the New Priestly Order under Jesus is much superior to the ancient Levitical Order!

CHAPTER 10

JESUS IN THE HOLY OF HOLIES

In the eighth chapter of *Hebrews*, the author gives us an idea of the state of affairs in Heaven.

Jesus is now our High Priest, seated at the right hand of God. He is serving as High Priest in the Heavenly Sanctuary, made by the Hand of God. As every high priest has to have something to offer, He offered His own Blood on Calvary once for all.

Then the author tells us something shocking but true:

"8:4 For if he were on earth, he would not be a priest at all".[119]

In Heaven, Jesus is High Priest seated at God's right hand. But, on earth, He would never have been even Priest!

That sounds unbelievable: yet, that's the truth!

You wonder why?

Well, He would not have been qualified simply because He was NOT born in the Tribe of Levi, but in the Tribe of Judah! As

---

[119] Hebrews 8:4.

we have already seen, only male members of the Tribe of Levi could enter the Priesthood!

Modern-day political leaders are now speaking about a New World Order. The New World Order they want to inaugurate, however, will usher in the reign of the Antichrist.

Jesus, on the other hand, has initiated a New High Priestly Order to present His Holy Blood as a Sacrifice for all who come to Him and confess Him as their Personal Saviour and Lord!

Another way in which Jesus's High Priesthood is superior to that of the Levitical Order concerns the sanctuary in which they serve.

The earthly tabernacle in which the Levitical High Priests served was built by men according to the model that God showed to Moses on the mountain. It was, however, only a representation of the Heavenly Tabernacle.

Jesus, on the other hand, is officiating in the Heavenly Tabernacle - the Archetype of the earthly one!

Consequently, Jesus *"has obtained **a more excellent ministry**, by so much as he is also the mediator of **a better covenant**, which on **better promises** has been given as law."*[120]

---

[120] Hebrews 8:6, emphasis added.

The above Scriptures show that, in every area, Jesus's High Priesthood is far better than that of the Levitical Order.

Indeed, *"if that first covenant had been faultless, then no place would have been sought for a second"*.[121]

It's logical that, had the first Covenant been perfect, there would have been no point in instituting another one.

It was precisely because of its imperfection that God made the following promise:

"8:10 "For this is the covenant that I will make with the house of Israel.

After those days," says the Lord;

---

[121] Hebrews 8:7.

"*I will put my laws into their mind,*

I will also write them on their heart.

I will be their God,

and they will be my people.

8:11 They will not teach every man his fellow citizen,

and every man his brother, saying, 'Know the Lord,'

for all will know me,

from the least of them to the greatest of them.

8:12 For I will be merciful to their unrighteousness."

I will remember their sins and lawless deeds no more."[122]

Based on the above Scriptures, in what sense would the New Covenant be different from the Old?

In the Old, God's Law was written on stone tablets. In the New, God's Law would be written in people's minds and hearts.

In the New, God would be King and the people would be His subjects.

In the Old Covenant, people went to the synagogues to hear the Word of God taught by doctors of the Law and rabbis.

---

[122] Hebrews 8:10-12.

In the New, nobody would have to teach the Word: God's people would intuitively know it – from the smallest to the greatest!

Ultimately, God would forget completely His people's sins and remember them no more.

As we have seen, there is not one single area in which the Old Covenant can be said to be better than the New!

"8:13 In that he says, "A new covenant," he has made the first old. But that which is becoming old and grows aged is near to vanishing away."[123]

The above Scriptures make it crystal clear that, now that the New Covenant has been instituted, the Old must disappear.

It's obvious that there cannot be two Covenants in effect simultaneously! If such was the case, the people would be in confusion. And God is not a God of confusion but of order![124] Imagine a Democratic Administration and a Republican Administration governing the U.S simultaneously!

In the Gospels, Jesus confirmed that by means of two parables, taught successively:

"No one puts a piece from a new garment on an old garment, or else he will tear the new,

---

[124] 1 Corinthians 14:33.

and also the piece from the new will not match the old."[125]

"5:37 No one puts new wine into old wineskins, or else the new wine will burst the skins, and it will be spilled, and the skins will be destroyed. 5:38 But new wine must be put into fresh wineskins, and both are preserved."[126]

The lesson He wanted to teach us is that we cannot mix the Old Covenant and the New.

Notice also that it is the new wine that bursts the old wineskin. That is, the New Covenant makes the Old obsolete!

---

[125] Luke 5:36.
[126] Luke 5:37-38.

CHAPTER 11

THE OLD VERSUS THE NEW

The author now details the way the office of the High Priest functions in the Tabernacle, opposing the Old Covenant to the New.

The earthly Tabernacle was a portable structure that God commanded Moses to build according to the precise model He showed him on Mount Sinai. During their forty-year wandering in the desert, God wanted to have a Place where He could dwell among His People.

The Tabernacle consisted of three sections: the Outer Court, the Holy Place and the Holy of Holies.

The Outer Court was where the people stood with their sacrifices. In it, were a brazen altar[127] on which animal sacrifices were burned and a laver[128] – a receptacle from which the Priest drew water to wash his hands and feet before entering the Tabernacle.

---

[127] Exodus 27:1-8.
[128] Exodus 30:17-21.

The Holy Place contained a golden lampstand[129], a table and the show bread.[130] That was where the Priest officiated.

Beyond the veil in the Holy Place, were a golden altar of incense and the Ark of the Covenant, overlaid with gold.

The Ark of the Covenant contained three very important items: the manna in a golden pot, the Tablets of the Covenant and Aaron's rod that had budded.

What is interesting is that every detail of the Tabernacle is related to Jesus in one way or another.

---

[129] Exodus 25:31-40.
[130] Hebrews 9:2.

So do the three items in the Ark of the Covenant.

The manna was that special food God sent down from Heaven to feed the Israelites who grumbled because they ran short of food in the desert.

One day, Jesus's detractors were boasting about their fathers who had eaten manna in the desert.

Refuting them, Jesus said: *"I am the bread of life. Whoever comes to me will not be hungry, and whoever believes in me will never be thirsty."*[131]

---

[131] John 6:35.

The Tablets of the Covenant represented the Word of God carved in stone. But Jesus, in His earthly ministry, was the Word of God Incarnate.[132] Now in Heaven He is the Living Word of God.

"[8] On the next day, Moses went into the Tent of the Testimony; and behold, Aaron's rod for the house of Levi had sprouted, budded, produced blossoms, and bore ripe almonds."[133]

One day, when the Israelites were still wandering in the desert, there arose a great rebellion against Moses and Aaron, his brother.

---

[132] John 1:1-18.
[133] Numbers 17:8.

God commanded Moses to ask the chiefs of the children of Israel to bring each a rod and to write their names on their respective rods. Moses did as commanded. He also wrote Aaron's name on the rod belonging to the tribe of Levi.

God then commanded Moses to place the twelve rods in the Tent of Meeting near the Ark of the Covenant where He used to meet with Moses. He would cause the rod of the one He had chosen to bud as an evidence to the people.

Moses followed God's instructions to the last letter.

"*8 On the next day, Moses went into the Tent of the Testimony; and behold, Aaron's rod*

for the house of Levi had sprouted, budded,
produced blossoms, and bore ripe
almonds. ⁹ *Moses brought out all the rods*
from before Yahweh to all the children of
Israel. They looked, and each man took his
rod."¹³⁴

On the next day, not only had Aaron's dead rod budded: it had also blossomed and borne ripe almonds! What a proof God had given to the Israelites that it was the Tribe of Levi He had chosen to serve in the priesthood!

What relationship does this have with Jesus?

Just like Aaron's dead rod budded, blossomed and produced fruit, so did Jesus

---

¹³⁴ Numbers 17:8-9.

die, rise from the dead and is still "begetting" children for God!¹³⁵

Moreover, in the Gospel of John, Jesus says:

"15:1 I am the true vine, and my Father is the farmer. 15:2 Every branch in me that doesn't bear fruit, he takes away. Every branch that bears fruit, he prunes, that it may bear more fruit. 15:3 You are already pruned clean because of the word which I have spoken to you. 15:4 Remain in me, and I in you. As the branch can't bear fruit by itself, unless it remains in the vine, so neither can you, unless you remain in me. 15:5 I am the vine. You are the branches. He who remains in me, and I in him, the same bears much fruit, for apart

---

[135] John 1:12-13.

from me you can do nothing. 15:6 If a man doesn't remain in me, he is thrown out as a branch, and is withered; and they gather them, throw them into the fire, and they are burned."[136]

In the above Scriptures, Jesus compares Himself to a vine and we, believers, to its branches. To bear fruit, we must remain attached to the vine. If we are severed from it, we die. Cut off from Jesus, we die spiritually!

As we have seen, the three articles kept in the Ark of the Covenant – the manna, the Tablets of the Law and Aaron's rod – all represent Jesus!

---

[136] John 15:1-6.

On the Ark of the Covenant, there were two cherubim, having six wings each: two to cover their face, two for cover their feet – out of reverence – and two to fly.[137]

Every day, the Priests entered the Holy Place to offer sacrifices for the people.

But, only once a year – on the Day of Atonement, Yom Kippur – could the High Priest enter the Holy of Holies to make atonement for the people's sins.

With regard to this ritual, the author of *Hebrews* tells us a few interesting things:

*"9:9 which is **a symbol of the present age**, where gifts and sacrifices are offered that are*

---

[137] Isaiah 6:2.

incapable, concerning the conscience, of making the worshipper perfect; 9:10 *being only (with meats and drinks and various washings) fleshly ordinances,* **imposed until a time of reformation.**"[138]

- The rituals practised in the Old Covenant period was only a "symbol of the present age".
- They were incapable of rendering the worshippers' conscience perfect.
- They had been "imposed until a time of reformation.

In other words, they were inefficient but had been established as an interim measure, pending a better and more efficacious

---

[138] Hebrews 9:9-10, emphasis added.

formula to make atonement and cleanse people's consciences of sin and the remembrance thereof.

That "time of reformation" was to come when Jesus would be established as High Priest in the Heavenly Tabernacle!

"9:11 But Christ having come as a high priest of the coming good things, through the greater and more perfect tabernacle, not made with hands, that is to say, not of this creation, 9:12 nor yet through the blood of goats and calves, but through his own blood, entered in once for all into the Holy Place, having obtained eternal redemption."[139]

---

[139] Hebrews 9:11-12.

In the two verses quoted above, the author summarizes beautifully what Jesus has come to accomplish.

Once Jesus had ascended to Heaven, the Father established Him as High Priest in the Holy of Holies. This is not a Tabernacle made by the hands of men, but by God, Himself. He got in not through the blood of an animal, but through His own sinless Blood. He has obtained an eternal redemption for all those who believe in Him and confess Him as personal Saviour and Lord. His High Priesthood will last forever!

Under the Old Covenant, animals' blood was poured to sanctify the flesh. But, Jesus's

Blood, purifies the soul, cleansing the conscience of all sins![140]

Jesus has, thus, become the sole Mediator of a New Covenant. He has, by His Sacrifice on the Cross, obtained a complete redemption from all transgressions committed under the Old Covenant. Consequently, those who had been righteous under the Old Covenant, might obtain the inheritance they had been looking for.[141]

We shall see that when we study chapter 11 of *Hebrews*.

---

[140] Hebrews 9:13.
[141] See my book *"Death Demystified"*.

The author now brings in the discussion another very important and pertinent argument.

Whenever a person expresses his last wish via a will or a testament, the dispositions of the will are ineffectual as long as he lives. It is only *after* his death that the will comes into force.

"9:16 For where a last will and testament is, there must of necessity be the death of him who made it. 9:17 For a will is in force where there has been death, for it is never in force while he who made it lives."[142]

---

[142] Hebrews 9:16-17.

That is yet another reason why Jesus had to die — so that the New Testament — signed by His Blood - could become effectual![143]

Even the First Testament was inaugurated with blood. After Moses had read all the Commandments God had given him, he sprinkled the blood of calves and goats — mixed with water, scarlet wool and hyssop on the Tablets of the Law and all the assembly.

He also sprinkled with blood the Tabernacle and all the vessels used for the service. He had to do that because, according to the Law, blood was an essential cleansing agent.[144]

---

[143] See my book *"Bought and Bonded by Blood"*.
[144] Hebrews 9:22.

If the earthly Tabernacle and its vessels had to be purified with blood, how much more did the Heavenly Sanctuary have to be purified - but with a much more potent Blood! That is yet another reason why Jesus had to shed His Holy Blood on the Cross!

However, unlike the Levitical Priests who had to sacrifice an animal each time they entered the Tent of Meeting, Jesus shed His Blood only once for its effect is everlasting!

Anyway, Jesus could not have died over and over to offer a Blood Sacrifice for *"it is appointed to men to die once and, after this, judgment."*[145]

---

[145] Hebrews 9:27.

However, He is getting ready to come a second time – not to suffer, die and rise again – but to take His Church home with Him! That glorious event will see the rapture of all those who look up to Him for their eternal salvation!

CHAPTER 12

EXHORTATION TO BELIEVERS

Quite a number of things have, by now, been made clear. Let us make a synthesis of all that before we move forward.

God gave the Law to Moses with a view to making His People pure and perfect. To make this possible, He showed Moses the model of a structure on the Mountain and commanded him to build a similar Tent so that He could meet with His People therein.

He established a Priesthood through the Tribe of Levi. Only male members of that family could officiate in that Tent, called Tabernacle.

The Priests were to offer animal sacrifices to make propitiation for the people's sins.

However, that earthly Priesthood was inefficient to cleanse people's consciences and bring them to salvation.

God, therefore, sent Jesus. He "prepared" a Body for Jesus who offered Himself as a Sacrifice, saying:

"Behold, I have come (in the scroll of the book it is written of me)

to do your will, O God"[146]

Jesus came in the flesh, suffered at the hands of mortal and sinful men, was crucified, died, rose again and ascended to Heaven.

Heaven is the Archetype of the earthly Tabernacle. Having shed His Blood only once on the Cross to wash away our sins for good, He is now our High Priest in the Heavenly Holy of Holies.

As the author puts it: *"For the law, having a shadow of the good to come, not the very image of the things"*.[147]

---

[146] Hebrews 10:7.
[147] Hebrews 10:1.

The Law *was* but a shadow: the reality *is* in Christ!

After having laid a foundation with his long theological discourse, the author adopts a down-to-earth tone to give us a few applications from it.

He starts with the exhortation *"Let us consider how to provoke one another to love and good works"*.[148]

His first plea is that we, believers, encourage one another to love one another and to practise good works.

---

[148] Hebrews 10:24.

This is in line with what Jesus, Himself, taught in the Gospels when He said: *"You shall love your neighbor as yourself."*[149]

As for practising good works, the Apostle Paul also taught the same thing: *"For we are his workmanship, created in Christ Jesus for good works, which God prepared before that we would walk in them."*[150]

Besides, God, Himself, through the Apostle John gives us a very good reason for that: *"Blessed are the dead who die in the Lord from now on.*

---

[149] Mark 12:31.
[150] Ephesians 2:10.

*"Yes," says the Spirit, "that they may rest from their labors; **for their works follow with them**."*[151]

The next encouragement he gives us is not to neglect our assembling together, especially as the Day of Jesus's Return draws near.

"... not forsaking our own assembling together, as the custom of some is, but exhorting one another; and so much the more, as you see the Day approaching."[152]

The believers in the Early Church persevered in four important things: fellowship, the

---

[151] Revelation: 14:13, emphasis added.
[152] Hebrews 10:25.

189

Apostles' teaching, breaking of bread and prayer.[153]

As a result of that, everyday new believers were added to the Church and the Lord worked all sorts of miracles through the hands of the Apostles.

There is power in unity. By exhorting us not to neglect our gathering together, the author wants us to grow individually as well as corporately. Thus, the Lord can work mightily among us.

Next, the author warns us against sinning willfully:

---

[153] Acts 2:42.

"10:26 For if we sin willfully after we have received the knowledge of the truth, there remains no more a sacrifice for sins, 10:27 but a certain fearful expectation of judgment, and a fierceness of fire which will devour the adversaries."

Once we have received the truth through faith in Jesus, we must not sin willfully. Otherwise, there will be no more sacrifice to redeem us, Jesus having already offered the very best sacrifice possible! The only alternative left will be the Lake of Fire, prepared not for us but for the devil.

Far from me to contradict the Word of God. But we remember the Prodigal Son. He left his father's house with his share of the inheritance, went to the city, squandered his money with friends and prostitutes until he was broke and became a swine-keeper.

But, one day, he made an introspection and resolved to go back to his father. Meanwhile, the latter had been hoping his son would return one day.

When he saw his son in the distance, he ran to welcome him back. He completely rehabilitated him and gave a feast in his honour.[154]

This is just a brief summary of this beautiful story that speaks of fatherly love.

---

[154] Luke 15:11-32.

The other example I can quote is the murderer crucified beside Jesus. While the other brigand was cursing and provoking Jesus, the repentant one turned to Jesus and asked Him to remember him when He would come in His Kingdom.

And what did Jesus respond?

"I tell you, today you will be with me in Paradise."[155]

The reason I have made reference to these two cases is to say that God is merciful. His mercy endures forever.[156]

It's never too late to come to Jesus. Even if, because of life circumstances, we have

---

[155] Luke 23:43.
[156] Psalm 136:1-9.

drifted away from God, it's never too late to come back to Him in repentance.

But, if we have gone so far as denying Jesus completely and retuning to our old pagan gods, then I'm afraid there's no further possibility of recovery!

A word of caution, though: the above is my personal understanding of the Word of God and must not be taken for an absolute truth. God is Sovereign: only He knows who is saved and who is not!

To support his idea, the author refers to the Mosaic Law. Anybody transgressing it was unceremoniously put to death upon the testimony of two or three witnesses.

If such was the case for breaking Moses's Law, then think of the seriousness of despising Jesus's Blood Sacrifice:

"10:29 How much worse punishment, do you think, will he be judged worthy of, who has trodden underfoot the Son of God, and has counted the blood of the covenant with which he was sanctified an unholy thing, and has insulted the Spirit of grace?"[157]

Despising the Blood Sacrifice of Jesus and insulting the Spirit of grace will entail God's judgment for:

"Vengeance belongs to me," says the Lord, "I will repay."[158]

---

[157] Hebrews 10:29.
[158] Hebrews 10:30.

And the author couples this with the following very severe words:

"It is a fearful thing to fall into the hands of the living God."[159]

Lest we take for nothing the Holy Sacrifice Jesus offered for us on the Cross, let us heed those eminently austere words of warning!

---

[159] Hebrews 10:31.

CHAPTER 13

LET'S RUN THE RACE

Having shown us a catalogue of heroes and heroines of Faith in chapter 11 of the Epistle, the author now exhorts us to follow their example and walk in faith, too.

"12:1 Therefore let us also, seeing we are surrounded by so great a cloud of witnesses, lay aside every weight and the sin which so easily entangles us, and let us run with patience the race that is set before us, 12:2 looking to Jesus, the author and perfecter of

faith, who for the joy that was set before him endured the cross, despising its shame, and has sat down at the right hand of the throne of God."[160]

Just like the Apostle Paul in many of his Epistles, the author – who may be Paul, himself, according to some Bible scholars – uses the analogy of a race in which we are engaged.[161]

He likens us, believers, to athletes running a race while, all around us, the stadium is crowded with heroic spectators, the "cloud of witnesses".

---

[160] Hebrews 12:1-3.
[161] 1 Corinthians 9:24. Galatians 5:7. Philippians 3:14. Colossians 3:23. 2 Timothy 4:7.

Imagine we are running a race under the "expert" gaze of pioneer "runners" like Abel, Abraham, Isaac, Jacob, Moses, Rahab, Samson and so on!

We have seen how, during a football match, the fans play a very important role as they clap, cheer and boo. This motivates the players to give their best. Some commentators call the crowd of supporters at a regular football match, "The Twelfth Man" in the team – so vital is their role!

Likewise, during the Olympics, before the high-jumper or the pole-jumper take their chance, they invite the crowd of spectators to clap rhythmically and in unison because that boosts them.

In the same way, if we imagine the great heroes and heroines of faith are watching us, applauding, what a boost that will be to us!

No runner can hope to win a race if he is burdened with a load! He has, first, to lay down his load or get rid of that fetter to which he is chained.

So, we, too, must get rid of every sin that so easily binds us and run our race, unencumbered.

Our best Witness or Spectator, though, is Jesus! He also, when He was on earth, ran His race. Even the prospect of having to face the Cross did not deter Him. His motivation was the joy that lay beyond the Cross where, once the ordeal was over, He would be enthroned with His Father.

In running His race, He set an example for us to follow. However, we do not have to struggle with sin to bleeding point as He did in Gethsemane.[162] Our race is, therefore, a much easier one.

THE NEED TO DISCIPLINE

"12:7 It is for discipline that you endure. God deals with you as with children, for what son is there whom his father doesn't discipline? 12:8 But if you are without discipline, of

---

[162] Matthew 26:36. Mark 14:32.

which all have been made partakers, then are you illegitimate, and not children. 12:9 Furthermore, we had the fathers of our flesh to chasten us, and we paid them respect. **Shall we not much rather be in subjection to the Father of spirits, and live?** *12:10 For they indeed, for a few days, punished us as seemed good to them; but he for our profit, that we may be partakers of his holiness. 12:11 All chastening seems for the present to be not joyous but grievous; yet afterward it yields the peaceful fruit of righteousness to those who have been exercised thereby."*[163]

Now the author comes to the question of discipline.

---

[163] Hebrews 12:7-12, emphasis added.

Every father disciplines his child. God, too, disciplines us because He treats us as His children. If He does not discipline us, then we are not His legitimate children – but bastards![164]

When we were kids, our fathers disciplined us for our own good. They wanted us to be subjected to them so that we might become good members of the society.

How much more should we, then, submit to our Heavenly Father's discipline to partake of His Holiness!

"12:11 All chastening seems for the present to be not joyous but grievous; yet afterward

---

[164] Hebrews 12:8 (KJV).

it yields the peaceful fruit of righteousness to those who have been exercised thereby."[165]

When, as children, we were punished by our parents, it caused us pain. But, later on, when we had grown up, we saw the good it did us.

Having been a high school teacher for fifty-two years, I can testify to that. When I started in the 1960s, corporal punishment was allowed. I have, therefore, punished quite a number of boys and girls.

But, later on, when they had become teachers, themselves, police officers, doctors, nurses, models, many have I met who expressed their gratitude to me. Among my former pupils, I have even had two barristers, three

---

[165] Hebrews 12:11.

Parliamentarians and ... a Miss Mauritius who was, thereafter, elected Miss World International in 2014!

All praise and glory to Jesus!

If we, human beings, chasten our children and pupils for their good, how much more our Heavenly Father will chasten us for our perfection!

That chastening should serve to encourage us to be bold and strong so that we may pursue peace with everybody, right living and sanctification *"without which no man will see the Lord"*.[166]

---

[166] Hebrews 12:14.

We must not be like Esau who despised his birthright and sold it to his brother Jacob for a meal of lentils.[167] Later on, when he realized his great mistake, he tearfully pleaded to have his birthright restored. But it was all to no avail.

THE TWO MOUNTAINS

To contrast the Old Covenant with the New, the author alludes to two mountains.

The first mountain was Mount Sinai. That

---

[167] Genesis 25:29-34; 27:30-40.

Mountain was in the desert. When Moses ascended the Mountain to receive the Tablets of the Law, God gave him very strict orders. The Mountain had to be fenced off. Nobody was to draw near. Any animal touching it was put to death. The thunder rolled, the lightning flashed, voices and the sound of trumpet resounded.

The spectacle was so frightening that even the great Moses, himself, said: "*I am terrified and trembling.*"[168]

That Mountain represented the Old Covenant which was characterized by the Law and which was ratified by the blood of animals.

---

[168] Hebrews 12:21.

That is not the Mountain that we, Christians, have come to!

The second Mountain is Mount Zion which is the "City of the Living God" – the New Jerusalem.[169]

While Mount Sinai kept people away for it and inspired fear and terror, the New Jerusalem extends an invitation to all:

"All those whom the Father gives me will come to me. He who comes to me I will in no way throw out."[170]

---

[169] Galatians 4: Revelation 21:1-2.
[170] John 6:37.

While the Old Covenant was based on the Law and condemnation, the New Covenant, Mount Zion, is founded on love and grace.

In contrast to the Old Covenant that was ratified by the blood of animals, the New Covenant was inaugurated by the shedding of Jesus's holy Blood.

To sum it all, the New Covenant is by far superior to the Old at all levels!

In establishing so many contrasts between the Old Covenant and the New, the author was, first of all, trying to persuade his Hebrew audience of the need to make the shift from the Law to Grace – from condemnation to salvation.

The author now gives a severe warning:

"12:25 See that you don't refuse him who speaks. For if they didn't escape when they refused him who warned on the Earth, how much more will we not escape who turn away from him who warns from heaven, 12:26 whose voice shook the earth then, but now he has promised, saying, "Yet once more I will shake not only the earth, but also the heavens."[171]

He reminds his readers that those who refused to listen to God when He spoke to them from the Mountain were punished. If now, they do not heed Him when He speaks from His Throne in Heaven, they can expect a much harsher punishment.

---

[171] Hebrews 12::25-26.

When He spoke from the Mountain, the earth shook. This time, if they don't listen, He will shake not only the earth, but the heavens, too!

This is quite understandable because, through the New Covenant, He is offering the very best – the quintessence of His Love!

CHAPTER 14

THE SPIRITUAL HALL OF FAMERS

Now we are in chapter 11 of *Hebrews*. It is entirely dedicated to the subject of Faith. We know how vital faith is with regard to our relationship to God. We can never speak about Faith without, at least once, referring to *Hebrews* chapter 11! It is a foundational chapter.

When the Church had entered the Dark Ages and all kinds of false doctrines had corrupted it, God used a man called Martin Luther[172] (1483-1546) to revive it. The Scripture that God used to trigger this revival which become known as the Great Reformation was:

"*... but the righteous will live by his faith.*"[173]

This verse is so important in the Bible that it is repeated in three other places: Romans 1:17, Galatians 3:11 and Hebrews 10:38.

The structure of this chapter is very simple and linear. It starts with a description of Faith, then mentions a number of great Bible

---

[172] Hillerbrand, Hans J.. "Martin Luther". Encyclopedia Britannica, 12 Sep. 2024, https://www.britannica.com/biography/Martin-Luther. Accessed 29 September 2024.
[173] Habakkuk 2:4.

characters – male and female – who applied it to their lives and who, at the end of their journey, received their reward.

For a study of these heroes and heroines, you may go to *"Learn Religions"*.[174]

For our part, because of the scope of this book, we shall refer only to a few of them because of their relative importance in the Bible and because of the exceptional experiences they had with God – although all of them are worth mentioning.

But first of all, let us see how the author defines Faith:

---

[174] Fairchild, Mary. "Heroes of Faith in the Book of Hebrews." Learn Religions, Aug. 29, 2024, learnreligions.com/hebrews-chapter-11-heroes-of-faith-700176. Accessed 29 September 2024.

"Now faith is assurance of things hoped for, proof of things not seen."[175]

To exercise faith, we must, first of all, have an assurance. The French Bible "Louis Segond" says *"une ferme assurance"* – a firm assurance!

Our assurance must be based on the Word of God for what He says, He will do it. He is not a man to lie:

"God is not a man, that he should lie, nor a son of man, that he should repent. Has he said, and he won't do it? Or has he spoken, and he won't make it good?"[176]

---

[175] Hebrews 11:1.
[176] Numbers 23:19.

That assurance must be *in* something. It's like shooting an arrow: our aim must be to hit the bull's eye. We must be focused on the subject of our assurance.

The other important aspect of faith is that the end result must be unseen to the human eye.

If we already see the result with our physical eyes or if it has already materialized, this is not faith.

The thing we are expecting and hoping for must not exist *yet* in the physical world. But we must believe it exists in the spiritual world and that, in response to our faith, God, in His Sovereignty, will make it happen – *if it is according to His will!*

This last detail is of the utmost importance: it's always God's will that eventually gets done!

Even Jesus, when He taught His disciples how to pray, included the words: *"Let your Kingdom come.* ***Let your will be done,*** *as in heaven, so on earth".*[177]

Also, when the Cup presented itself to Him in the Garden of Gethsemane, He prayed: *"Father, if you are willing, remove this cup from me. Nevertheless,* ***not my will, but yours, be done".***[178]

Faith is an axiom. It is the basic concept that we must acknowledge when we approach

[177] Matthew 6:10, emphasis added.
[178] Luke 22:42, emphasis added.

God. We must accept that He exists and that the world has been created by Him.

Genesis, The Book of the Beginnings, itself, does not debate or question the existence God: it simply affirms it:

"In the beginning God created the heavens and the earth."[179]

Indeed, there would not have been a Creation if there had not been a Creator!

We just have to believe it and move on from there.

But that is not all there is to Faith.

The Apostle James, in his Epistle, adds other requirements, namely that our faith must be

---

[179] Genesis 1:1.

for a good purpose – not for a selfish one[180] –
and it must be coupled with works.[181]

As this is not the aim of this book, we are not
going to delve here into what James says.
Besides, it is a highly debated subject.

In our discussion about the subject of Faith,
we are *not* promoting the doctrine commonly
known as "*Name it and Claim it*!

This false doctrine is closer to the New Age
cult than to Christianity. It is also known as
the "*Word of Faith*" and the "*Prosperity
Gospel*".

The bottom line is that it equates faith with
wealth. If you have enough faith, you can call

---

[180] James 4:2-3.
[181] James 2:14. 2:24.

into existence prosperity in the form of money, cars, yachts, private jets and so on. Its promoters claim that God wants us to be prosperous and happy all the time.

Now that we have seen the definition of Faith, let us look at some of the heroes and heroines mentioned in *Hebrews 11*.

ABEL

Why do we start with Abel?

Well, even the author of *Hebrews* starts with him. He is also the first crime victim and the first martyr in the whole history of the world and, incidentally, his name begins … with an A!

These facts are more than enough to justify his first place in the Hall of Fame of Faith.

Who was Abel?

Abel was the second son born to the first couple, Adam and Eve. His elder brother was Cain.

Cain was a planter while Abel was a shepherd.

One day, they both brought a sacrifice to God. Cain gave of his crop while Abel offered a few of the first-born from his flock.[182]

---

[182] Genesis 4:4.

God was pleased with Abel's sacrifice but rejected Cain's.[183]

Out of jealousy and anger, Cain took his younger brother into the field and murdered him there.

Yet, God had warned him about sin *"crouching at the door"* and had advised him to *"do well"*.[184]

As a result of that, God cursed Cain.[185]

Many have questioned why God accepted Abel's sacrifice but rejected Cain's.

Some have concluded that it was because Abel offered a blood sacrifice for he had to

---

[183] Genesis 4:2-8.
[184] Genesis 4:7.
[185] Genesis 4:11.

kill the animal(s) he offered and shed its (their) blood.

Cain, on the other hand, offered a vegetal sacrifice. Hence, no blood was involved.

While this *may* have been the case, the Bible, nevertheless, does not say anything of that ilk![186]

However, it is true that God demands the first fruit of anything we produce – crop, animal or money.

In this aspect, Abel did right for it is explicitly said that he offered "*some of the firstborn of his flock and of its fat.*"[187]

---

[186] Genesis 4:1-8.
[187] Genesis 4:4.

God may also have judged the brothers by the attitude of their hearts in their giving. Abel may have offered his sacrifice wholeheartedly while his brother may have given his grudgingly!

Nevertheless, all this is mere speculation.

The bare fact is that God is sovereign and does whatever He wills!

Anyway, Abel offered His sacrifice in faith and has, today, received his reward in Heaven.

ENOCH

The second example we are going to consider is a man called Enoch.

We don't know much about him: the Bible does not speak lengthily about him.

We are told he was the son of Jared.[188] At 65, he became the father of Methuselah – the man who lived the longest: 969 years![189]

After Methuselah's birth, Enoch lived three hundred more years during which time, he begot more sons and daughters.[190]

Altogether, he lived 365 years.

Enoch was a very special person. His case is simply outstanding. His achievement?

"Enoch walked with God, and he was not, for God took him."

---

[188] Genesis 5:19.
[189] Genesis 5:21.
[190] Genesis 5:22.

He was so upright and God-fearing a man that he knew no death: God simply took him up to Heaven!

He was the first of only two men who were taken up to Heaven without experiencing death – the second man being Elijah, the prophet.[191]

As Enoch was the very first man ever to be lifted to Heaven and as this is related in *Genesis*, the Book of Beginnings, we can conclude that this lays the foundation of the doctrine of the Rapture which is contested by many on the basis that the word "Rapture" does not appear in the Bible.

---

[191] 2 Kings 2:1-18.

Another doctrine that is contested for the same reason is that of the Trinity.

But, as the saying goes: "What's in a name?"

The fact that these two words do not appear in the Bible does not mean that the doctrines – the concepts for those who dislike Christianese – do *not* exist!

If we consider the number of things that exist even though their names are not found in the Bible!

Ever seen words like oxygen, heatwave, Venus, Mars, diabetes, high blood pressure, pizza, burger, hotdog, Wi-Fi, computer, mobile phone in the Bible?

And yet, they very much exist!

Some will argue that my examples are not of the same order as "Trinity" and "Rapture" because they are not spiritual or philosophical.

But see what the Bible says:

"... while we don't look at the things which are seen, but at the things which are not seen. ***For the things which are seen are temporal, but the things which are not seen are eternal."***[192]

The spiritual is much more important than the physical: the physical is visible but temporal and ephemeral; the spiritual is invisible but eternal.

---

[192] 2 Corinthians 4:18.

Anyhow, Enoch walked with God by faith and, eventually, received his prize.

<u>NOAH</u>

The next example we are going to consider is Noah.

Noah was another man who was upright and who walked with God. Though not perfect, he was blameless before his compatriots.

However, by that time, the world had become completely corrupt. Sin was rampant.[193]

---

[193] Genesis 6:9-1

So much so that God could bear it no longer: He resolved to destroy the world!

But God has a principle: He never destroys without first giving a warning! Moreover, He also gives a way out!

This is constantly seen in the Bible.

For example, He warned Abraham when He planned to destroy Sodom and Gomorrah. In Egypt, He warned Moses before He sent the Angel of Death to destroy the first-born of the Egyptians.

What about the present day?

Well, Jesus has given us multiple warnings in Luke 17:22-37, Luke 21:20-36, Matthew 24 and via a number of parables.

Also, the Apostles Paul and Peter have given many warnings regarding the destruction of this world.

God informed Noah that He would send a flood that would drown the whole world. But He instructed Noah to build a large ship according to the specifications He gave him. The ship – known as Noah's Ark – was to be a refuge for Noah, his family and animal species that God wanted to preserve.

What was formidable with Noah's faith was that it had never rained[194] when God told him He would send a flood!

Yet, Noah believed God and faithfully built his Ark as instructed. He warned the people

---

[194] Genesis 2:5.

of the impending catastrophe and the need to repent, but they mocked him.[195] What they found even more insane was that Noah was building his ship inland – away from the sea!

When the Ark was ready, God commanded Noah to get inside with the members of his immediate family and male and female species of animals so that they might be preserved.

When that was done, God closed the door of the Ark and sent down a flood that kept pouring for full forty days and nights.

The mockers came knocking on the door of the Ark, but it remained resolutely closed!

---

[195] 2 Peter 2:5.

Eventually, they all drowned whereas Noah and seven members of his family – his wife, three daughters and their husbands were safe and sound!

In the Gospel, Jesus warns us that, in the end times, the situation will be exactly as during the days of Noah.[196]

Except that now we don't have an Ark to take refuge in, but we have the Church[197] which is called the Body of Christ![198]

Jesus is building His Church – the global body of believers – which He is coming to

---

[196] Matthew 24:37-39.
[197] Matthew 16:18.
[198] 1 Corinthians 12:27.

rapture before Hell is set loose and the end comes.

To escape Doomsday, our only safe refuge is the Body of Christ.

How to integrate it?

We must repent of our sins, believe in Jesus and confess Him as our personal Saviour and Lord.

ABRAHAM

This man was first called Abram. Later, God changed his name to Abraham. His wife was called Sarai but God later changed it to Sarah.

For simplicity, I shall, in this section, only refer to them as Abraham and Sarah, the names by which they are best known.

This man also has a most wonderful testimony of faith.

He was old and his wife was old, too, and barren in the bargain! Consequently, they had no child.

One day, God appeared to Abraham and ordered him to leave his country and move to another land to which He would guide him. The land where God eventually led him was called Canaan which, from then on, was referred to as the Promised Land. Later on, this country became Israel, the country that has become the epicenter of all the world's geopolitical conflicts that we know today.

One day, Abraham was complaining to God about the fact that he was old and was about to die without having an heir.

God promised to give him a son through whom he would become the father of many nations.

Thinking that God's promise would not be realizable because of her old age and barrenness, Sarah suggested that he should beget a son for them through Hagar, an Egyptian slave woman in their service.

Abraham followed his wife's advice and a son was born to them whom they called Ismael.

But God reprimanded Abraham and told him that His promise concerned a son who would be born to him and his legitimate wife, Sarah.

In due time, God, indeed, gave them a son whom they called Isaac.

One day, God wanted to put Abraham's faith to the test. He asked the old man to offer Him Isaac as a burnt offering!

Just imagine the state of mind in which that must have put Abraham! Isaac was his only son and heir! He had begotten the child in his old age! God had told him that, through that son, he would become the father of many nations! And now God was asking him to offer the child to Him as a burnt offering!

How absurd it all looked! Why had God given him a son to ask that he be put to death? If Abraham sacrificed the child, what would be the probability of his having another one?

What would old Abraham do?

To sacrifice or not to sacrifice?

But see what the old man's reaction was:

"By faith, Abraham, being tested, offered up Isaac. Yes, he who had gladly received the promises was offering up his one and only son; 11:18 even he to whom it was said, "In Isaac will your seed be called;"* **11:19 concluding that God is able to raise up even from the dead.** Figuratively speaking, he also did receive him back from the dead."*[199]

Unbelievable! Just as Abraham had abandoned his home country and relatives to follow God to a foreign land without arguing, questioning or regretting, he conscientiously took the child up a mountain to sacrifice him.

---

[199]Hebrews 11:17-19, emphasis added.

However, just as Abraham's knife was about to slash open the child's throat, the angel of the LORD miraculously arrested his hand![200]

He showed Abraham a ram that had been caught in the bushes by its thorns.

Abraham released his son whom he had bound and sacrificed the ram in his place!

As the above Scriptures show, Abraham's faith lay in the confidence that God could raise his son from the dead, were he put to death.

And, in a sense, when Isaac was set free at the ultimate moment, it was as if God had, indeed, raised him from the dead!

---

[200] Genesis 22:15.

The important point is that Abraham demonstrated an incredible faith. He was put to the test on the basis of his faith and he brilliantly passed the test!

You will understand that the story of Abraham is too long and that we have limited ourselves to what is relevant to *Hebrews 11*.

MOSES

Who hasn't ever heard of Moses? Who doesn't know him?

Believers and non-believers alike must have heard of him. His name was made popular by the great movie *"The Ten Commandments"*.[201]

We are choosing Moses because of the major role he played in the Old Testament. He is, by far, the greatest figure in the Old Testament and one of the greatest in the entire Bible.

The whole story of Moses is told in *Exodus*, the second Book in the Bible.

But let us make a summary of it.

Moses was born as an Israelite slave boy in Egypt. In those days, the Pharaoh had ordered the murder of all male new-born Israelite

---

[201] Wikipedia: "The Ten Commandments": Epic religious drama film, produced, directed and narrated by Cecil B. DeMille and released in 1956. Accessed on 30 September 2024.

boys because he feared they might grow up, form an army and conquer Egypt.

Moses's mother put baby Moses in a basket and sent his sister to drop the basket on the River Nile. As the basket flowed down the River, Moses's sister discreetly followed it to know where it would land.

Downstream, Pharaoh's daughter was bathing in the company of her maids. When the basket drew near them, they picked it up and found the baby inside. Pharaoh's daughter decided to adopt him.

Moses's sister came out of her hiding and asked the Princess whether she wouldn't need a woman to nurse the baby.

The Princess having said yes, she went back home and brought ... her own mother! Thus, unbeknown to others, Moses was breastfed by his own mother!

Right from the beginning, it was the Hand of God that was guiding everything because He needed Moses for a very noble purpose.

To cut a long story short, later Moses killed and buried in the sand an Egyptian who was molesting a Hebrew.

The thing having been known, Moses fled and went to keep his father-in-law's flocks.

That was when God appeared to him in a burning bush and commissioned him to go back to Egypt and set the Hebrews free from Egyptian bondage.

That he successfully achieved by the mighty Hand of God.

As the story of Moses covers the whole Book of *Exodus,* it would be impossible to narrate it all here.

Also, the part of his life that is referred to in the Hall of Fame of Faith in *Hebrews* concerns the earlier part while he was in Egypt.

Let's see what the author of *Hebrews* says:

"By faith, Moses, when he had grown up, refused to be called the son of Pharaoh's daughter, 11:25 choosing rather to share ill treatment with God's people, than to enjoy the pleasures of sin for a time; 11:26 **accounting the reproach of**

Christ greater riches than the treasures of Egypt; for he looked to the reward. 11:27 By faith, he left Egypt, not fearing the wrath of the king; for he endured, as seeing him who is invisible."."[202]

There, was a man who was born as a slave, who grew up in the palace of the king of the most powerful kingdom on earth at that time, who received the best education of that time and who would later succeed the Pharaoh on the throne of Egypt, thus becoming the most powerful monarch of that time!

Yet, he chose to despise the riches of Egypt, preferring to side with God's people and share their miseries!

---

[202] Hebrews 11:24-27, emphasis added.

Was it madness? Nonsense? Foolishness? Lack of ambition?

Far from that: he considered *"the reproach of Christ greater riches than the treasures of Egypt; for he looked to the reward."*

Indeed, he understood that, in Jesus, there were infinitely greater riches than all the treasures of Egypt!

The choice he made was most judicious for the heavenly riches in Christ are eternal while those of Egypt would have been for a time only.

Also what motivated Moses in his choice was that he was looking forward to the reward:[203] an eternal reward stored in Heaven!

What a wonderful example we have in Moses! What motivation for us, modern-day believers!

The Apostle Paul exhorts us also to do the same thing:

"If then you were raised together with Christ, seek the things that are above, where Christ is, seated on the right hand of God. 3:2 Set your mind on the things that are above, not on the things that are on the earth."[204]

---

[203] Hebrews 11:26.
[204] Colossians 3:1-2.

RAHAB

There are many great women who played important parts in the Bible such as Sarah, Deborah, Esther and Ruth, to name but a few.

But the one we would like to talk about now is Rahab. Hers was a very unusual case.

Rahab was a prostitute in the City of Jericho. As such, she was undoubtedly rejected by her relatives and looked down upon by society.

Her infamous house was located on the ramparts protecting the City. That location was, no doubt, to keep her dirty activity away from the "respectable" society.

After Moses's death, young Joshua took over to lead the Israelites into Canaan. The first obstacle that stood before them was Jericho, a solidly barricaded City. It was, in fact, almost impregnable![205]

As a good commander, Joshua sent two spies into the City to reconnoiter the City and see how best to invade it.

As soon as the spies entered the City, the very first house they came to was Rahab's house precisely because it was located on the ramparts. Seeing therein a God-sent opportunity to save her close ones, she lodged the Hebrew spies in her house.

---

[205] Joshua 6:1-2.

But news soon reached the king of Jericho that two Hebrew spies had come to spy out the City and that they were in Rahab's house.

The king sent soldiers to ask Rahab to hand over the spies.

Meanwhile, the clever woman had hidden the spies under stalks of flax on the roof of her house.

She told the kings' soldiers that two men had, indeed, come to her place but she did not know where they had gone. At dusk, as the City gate was about to close, they had left without her knowing where they went. She asked the soldiers to hurry in order to catch them.

Then she must have told herself: "It's now or never!"

She went up on the roof and told the two spies:

"I know that Yahweh has given you the land, and that the fear of you has fallen on us, and that all the inhabitants of the land melt away before you. 2:10 For we have heard how Yahweh dried up the water of the Red Sea before you, when you came out of Egypt; and what you did to the two kings of the Amorites, who were beyond the Jordan, to Sihon and to Og, whom you utterly destroyed."[206]

---

[206] Joshua 2:9-10.

Confident that God had given Jericho to the Israelites, she begged the Hebrew spies to spare her family on the day of the battle.

Then, by means of a cord, she lowered the spies down the wall through the window.

In return for her precious assistance, the spies made a pledge with her.

They told her to tie a scarlet rope to her window as a landmark and, on the day of the invasion, to gather all the members of her family inside her house.

On the day of the battle, should a member of her family be killed outside her house, the Israelites would bear no blame for it. But they swore to spare all inside her house.

Then she ordered the spies to hurry and hide in the mountains for three days until the king's soldiers had returned. After that, they could safely go back to their army.

On the Israeli side, God gave Joshua a unique plan to bring down the walls of the City. You can read about it in Joshua chapter 6.

Once the walls had miraculously collapsed, the Israeli army invaded the City, killed everybody and burned the City.

However, in Rahab's house, the whole company was safe and sound! The two spies were asked to bring them out.

Thus, the Israelites had been faithful to their oath which they had sworn in return of Rahab's kindness to them.

Finally, Rahab accompanied the Israelites back, became one of them and married a man called Salmon.

But the best part of the story is that, down the generations, the great king David, his son Solomon and, eventually, Joseph would be born in that lineage!

That Joseph was the one who was betrothed to Mary, Jesus's mother, and who would later marry her.[207]

What a miracle in the life of Rahab, that former prostitute! What an unexpected but glorious consequence to the faith she

---

[207] Matthew 1:1-17: The Genealogy of Jesus.

exercised when she protected the Israeli spies!

There are so many lessons we can draw from the story of Rahab. But, in the context of *Hebrews* 11, suffice to say that today – like Abel, Abraham, Moses and so many other ancient heroes and heroines – she has also received her reward in eternity!

With such a vast number of heroes and heroines of faith in Bible story, the author of *Hebrews*, himself, says that "[...] *time would fail him*"[208] if he were to speak about them all in detail.

---

[208] Hebrews 11:32.

However, at the end of this chapter on the Heroes and Heroines of Faith, he says something very interesting:

"These all, having had testimony given to them through their faith, ***didn't receive the promise, 11:40 God having provided some better thing concerning us, so that apart from us they should not be made perfect.""*[209]

On the basis of their exceptional faith, all the heroes and heroines of old received *the promise of a reward but not the reward, itself!*

---

[209] Hebrews 11:39-40, emphasis added.

In other words, they were putting their indefectible faith in God, confident that He watches over His Word to perform it.[210]

That was quite in conformity with the definition the author gave of Faith at the beginning of the chapter – the assurance of things hoped for, the proof of things not seen.

But the most interesting thing the author says above is that God had, then, prepared something better so that they would not be made perfect *without us*!

In other words, God wanted us, New Testament believers, to partake of the reward with them. So, He kept the reward "in escrow", as it were, until Jesus had shed His

---

[210] Jeremiah 1:12.

Blood so we could also have our share of the reward!

What a good God we have and what a wonderful Saviour we have in Jesus!

CHAPTER 15

SPIRITUAL NUGGETS

The vulgarization of fast-food has made the word "nuggets" popular. It refers to little rounded pieces of fried chicken meat.

People – especially children – are very fond of them because of their crunchiness.

When I was a kid, people were not very well-off. Families were large and pastry was a luxury for many.

There used to be a cake called *"madrier"*.[211] It was a thick rectangular cake made of all bits and pieces of other cakes.

It had certain advantages: among others, it cost only a few cents and easily filled the stomach. So, a large family could easily have their fill with a few of those.

Without any offense meant, I like to say that, in the final chapter of *Hebrews*, the author offers his readers a platter of "nuggets".

Indeed, in that chapter, he touches briefly on a number of miscellaneous subjects to help us keep on track in our spiritual race.

---

[211] Large wooden beam used as building material.

BROTHERLY LOVE

(13:1)

Brotherly love is the very first "nugget" the author mentions.

This is quite understandable in so far as love is the very basis of Christianity. God gave us Jesus as an act of love:

"For God so loved the world, that he gave his one and only Son, that whoever believes in him should not perish, but have eternal life."[212]

---

[212] John 3:16.

Besides, it is one of the two Commandments Jesus gave us:

"One of the scribes came, and heard them questioning together. Knowing that he had answered them well, asked him, "Which commandment is the greatest of all?"

12:29 Jesus answered, "The greatest is, 'Hear, Israel, the Lord our God, the Lord is one: 12:30 you shall love the Lord your God with all your heart, and with all your soul, and with all your mind, and with all your strength.'* This is the first commandment. **12:31 The second is like this, 'You shall love your neighbor as yourself.'* There is no other commandment greater than these."**[213]

---

[213] Mark 12:28-31, emphasis added.

Brotherly love is much more important than we might think. See what the Apostle John says:

"He who doesn't love his brother remains in death. 3:15 Whoever hates his brother is a murderer, and you know that no murderer has eternal life remaining in him."[214]

HOSPITALITY

(13:2)

The author exhorts us to practise hospitality because some have received angels under their roof, unbeknown to them.

---

[214] 1 John 3:14-15.

This reminds us of Lot, Abraham's nephew, who were visited by two angels whom God had sent to warn him of the imminent destruction of Sodom where he lived.

We usually conceive angels as mighty spiritual winged beings – and, indeed, they are.

But the two angels who were sent to warn Lot appeared in human form. They had no wings and looked like any human being – so much so that the wicked inhabitants of Sodom wanted to have sex with them.

God is Sovereign. He may sometimes send an angel to our help in times of difficulty. But the angel may well come in human guise.

How many times have we been in a dangerous situation and a "stranger" *just happened to pass our way at that specific moment* to miraculously rescue us! And, once we had been rescued, the "stranger" just walked away without us knowing who he was, where he came from nor where he went!

"Aren't they [angels] *all serving spirits, sent out to do service for the sake of those who will inherit salvation?"*[215]

However, a word of caution: we must exercise discernment and not receive just any individual under our roof. People have become so wicked now that some evil-doer may pass himself – or herself – off as

---

[215] Hebrews 1:14.

somebody in need of food or shelter and take advantage of our hospitality.

PRISONERS

(13:3)

The author now wants his readers to remember those who are in prison and feel empathy for them.

During the first century AD, there were very severe persecutions against Christians and many were cast in prisons because of their faith.

Those who were free were exhorted to remember their less fortunate fellow believers in their prayers.

This exhortation applies to us also now. In many countries, Christians are mercilessly persecuted and thrown into prisons.

"Open Doors" is a site that regularly updates its watch list of countries where persecution against Christians is the fiercest. North Korea most often tops the list.

As we are already in the end times, persecution is going to get more and more severe.

We, who are free, have a duty towards our brothers and sisters who are facing persecution at the hands of increasing antagonistic groups. We must remember them in our prayers and ask God to stand with them in their ordeals.

MARRIAGE

(13:4)

We are now exhorted to keep the wedding bed undefiled.

God, Himself, instituted marriage when He brought Adam and Eve together in the Garden of Eden.[216]

---

[216] Genesis 2:24.

Marriage, therefore, is a sacred tie bonding a man and a woman together for life.[217] We must make sure we live up to our wedding vows.

But, today, the situation is turning bad. Not only divorce is rampant among the Christian community, but we are consenting to same sex marriages in violation of God's Law[218]. Some churches are even celebrating same sex marriages and ordaining homosexual priests and pastors!

All these are abominations to the LORD.

---

[217] 1 Corinthians 7:39.
[218] Leviticus 18:22. Leviticus 20:13. Romans 1:27.

LOVE OF MONEY

(13:5-6)

The author now guards us against the love of money.

The Apostle Paul, in writing to Timothy, says the following:

"For the love of money is a root of all kinds of evil. Some have been led astray from the faith in their greed, and have pierced themselves through with many sorrows."[219]

---

[219] 1 Timothy 6:10.

We often hear people "quote" this Scripture. But, in fact, most of the time, they misquote it for they say: "*Money* is the root of all evils".

The problem is not money per se but the love of it. This is called "cupidity".

For an excessive love for money, many have drifted away from the faith and caused a lot of misery to themselves and to their close ones.

Today, this warning is of the utmost importance because of the false doctrine called the "*Prosperity Gospel*" that has gained much ground in modern-day Christianity.

Basically, this false "Gospel" equates blessing with material wealth in terms of money, yachts, penthouses, private jets and so on.

Yet, God tells us: *"I will in no way leave you, neither will I in any way forsake you".*[220]

He is our Jehovah-Jireh, our Provider.

The Apostle Paul also tells us:

*"My God will supply every **need** of yours according to his **riches** in glory in Christ Jesus."*[221]

---

[220] Hebrews 13:5.
[221] Philippians 4:19, emphasis added.

God promises to supply our every need – not to satisfy the object of our every extravagance or covetousness!

Do we doubt His Word or the riches that are in Christ?

In the Sermon upon the Mount, Jesus says:

*"See the birds of the sky, that they don't sow, neither do they reap, nor gather into barns. Your heavenly Father feeds them. **Aren't you of much more value than they**?"*[222]

Let us, in faith, trust our Heavenly Father to supply our every need as He says He will.

---

[222] Matthew 6:26, emphasis added.

OBEDIENCE TO OUR LEADERS

(13:7-9)

"13:17 Obey your leaders and submit to them, for they watch on behalf of your souls, as those who will give account, that they may do this with joy, and not with groaning, for that would be unprofitable for you."[223]

The author now tells us that we should remember and obey our leaders – those who teach us the Word of God. We must obey them and imitate their faith. They are our spiritual role models. If those who have gone

---

[223] Hebrews 13:17.

on have received their reward, by imitating their faith, we will receive ours, as well.

Our leaders have a most important role to play. They feed us with spiritual food, watch over our souls and have to give a report thereof to God.

Consequently, we must behave towards them in such a way that they serve us joyfully and not grudgingly.

Jesus Christ is the same – yesterday, today and forever.[224]

What He has done for them, He will do for us, too.

---

[224] Hebrew 13:8

STRANGE TEACHINGS

(13:9)

The author also warns us not to get carried away by believing all sorts of doctrines. Our spiritual food must be founded in grace and not in pernicious doctrines that are more detrimental than beneficial.

Towards the close of his Letter, the author reminds us of the high privilege we enjoy in Jesus:

"13:10 We have an altar from which those who serve the holy tabernacle have no right to eat. 13:11 For the bodies of those animals, whose blood is brought into the holy place by the high priest as an offering for sin, are

burned outside of the camp..* *13:12 Therefore Jesus also, that he might sanctify the people through his own blood, suffered outside of the gate."*[225]

When pagans offer sacrifices to their gods in their temples, they eat the flesh once the blood has been poured.

That is why one element of the deliberations of the Council of Jerusalem was to warn us against eating food sacrificed to idols.[226]

Also, one of the false teachings of the false prophetess Jezebel in the Church at Thyatira was to make God's children eat meat

---

[225] Hebrews 13:10-12.
[226] Acts 15:20.

sacrificed to idols. For that, she incurred Jesus's severe reprimand.[227]

In the Old Testament, certain animals brought to the Temple could be eaten by the priests.

But the bodies of sin sacrifices were burned outside the camp.[228]

When Jesus was on trial before Pontius Pilate and the latter asked the crowd what he should do with Jesus, they shouted:

"Let him be crucified! [.....] May his blood be on us, and on our children!"[229]

---

[227] Revelation 2:20.
[228] Exodus 29:14; Leviticus 4:12; Numbers 19:3.
[229] Matthew 27:23, 25.

By so doing, they were committing a big sin and invoking a curse upon them and upon the City.

For that reason, Jesus, the sacrificial Lamb of God, had to be taken out of the City of Jerusalem to be crucified on Golgotha, "the Place of a Skull".[230]

That's why, in one of his final exhortations, the author tells his Hebrew readers:

"13:13 Let us therefore go out to him outside of the camp, bearing his reproach. 13:14 For we don't have here an enduring city, but we seek that which is to come."[231]

---

[230] John 19:17.
[231] Hebrews 13:13-14.

It's an invitation to them to leave the ancient Levitical Order of the Priesthood and place themselves under the High Priesthood of Jesus. Thus, they can hope for an eternal City which is the New Jerusalem in Heaven.

As all believers in Christ – Jews and Gentiles - have collectively become a royal priesthood,[232] the author extends to all of us the following invitation:

"13:15 Through him, then, let us offer up a sacrifice of praise to God[*] continually, that is, the fruit of lips which proclaim allegiance to his name."[233]

---

[232] 1 Peter 2:9.
[233] Hebrews 13:15.

PAUL, THE AUTHOR OR NOT?

In concluding the Letter, the author encourages his readers to pray for him and his companions (us) *"that I may be restored to you sooner."*[234]

Is that an indication that the author was in prison? Or was he simply prevented from visiting them for some other reason?

Who were the "us"?

As we said in the Preface, there are indications in the Epistle that the author must have been known to his readers.

---

[234] Hebrews 13:19.

Otherwise, how could he have asked them to pray for him so that he might be restored to them?

They would have to know who was asking them to pray for him, who could not be with them during that time and why. More importantly, how would they know if their prayers had been answered and the person in question had been restored to them?

The "anonymity" of the Epistle must have been a demonstration of humility on the part of the author in relation to the Supreme Grandeur of the Person he speaks of!!

Closer to the end, he says:

*"Know that **our brother** Timothy has been freed, with whom, if he comes shortly, I will see you."*[235]

Had Timothy also been in prison?

Another question arises: some say that the Epistle was written by the Apostle Paul. Did Paul not refer to Timothy as *"my son"*?[236]

But in the Scripture quoted above, the author refers to Timothy as *"our brother"*.

Is this an indication that Paul was not the author?

Some will argue that Paul – if he wrote the Epistle – could *not* have written: *"our son*

---

[235] Hebrews 13:23.
[236] 1 Timothy 1:1:2, 18.

Timothy" because Timothy did not have the same relationship with the others.

But then, he could have written "Timothy, my son and your brother".

The above questions and reflections were not meant to express any agreement or disagreement with those who support Paul's authorship but just to say that it could have been Paul as much as it could have *not* been Paul.

For my part, when God speaks, I listen; when He keeps quiet, I respect His silence.

I believe the author chose to remain anonymous because he wanted his readers to know the One written about - not the one doing the writing! His focus had to be on Jesus, the central Figure in this Epistle.

As John the Baptist put it so beautifully: *"He must increase, but I must decrease."*[237]

---

[237] John 3:30.

CHAPTER 16

CONCLUSION

Now that you have reached the end of the study of *Hebrews*, we are sure you will agree that this is the Queen of all Epistles – not only because of the style in which it is written but more especially because of the subject it deals with.

As we said in the Preface, *Hebrews* does not follow the pattern of the other Epistles. An Epistle being a Letter, it should normally begin by mentioning the name of the author or authors, the person or community to whom it is addressed and a salutation.

Its original beginning departs from that of the other Epistles – especially those written by Paul.

Instead, it starts by projecting on the scene the One who is the Beginning, the Source of everything: God.

The incipit is not without reminding us of that of *Genesis:* in both, God, the Creator is first and foremost.

In the very first sentence, the author projects onto the scene God and His Son Jesus.

To the perspicacious mind, it is obvious, from then on, that Jesus will be the Main Character in the scenario.

Like a film director or a cameraman, the author eclipses himself backstage and focuses the spotlight on Jesus.

With regard to the content also, the author does not tackle temporal problems like disputes within the church, food sacrificed to idols, marriage, church administration, false teachings and so on.

Instead, he demonstrates Jesus's superiority over everyone and everything the Hebrews held as elevated, eminent and worthy of reverence – angels, Moses, the Old Covenant and the Levitical Priesthood. They all pale before Him!!

Unlike the Gospels – especially the Synoptics – that present Jesus in His earthly role, the Epistle to the Hebrews presents Him as our High Priest in the Heavenly Tabernacle.

Gone are the days of His humiliation and of His suffering! Now, He is seated at God's right hand on His Heavenly Throne!

To gain access into the Heavenly Tabernacle and be elevated to such a high position, He has had to endure the ordeal of the Cross and shed His pure, sinless and holy Blood.

As opposed to the Levitical Priesthood that was temporary and transmissible, Jesus's

High Priesthood is forever and, hence, not transmissible.

In writing the Epistle to the Hebrews, the author aims:

- To present Jesus as God, the Creator.
- To show the superiority of Jesus over everyone and everything else.
- To mention a catalogue of some great men and women of God who walked by faith and who have received their eternal reward.
- To encourage his Jewish audience to make the shift from the Levitical Order to the New Order according to Melchizedek, inaugurated by Jesus.

- To exhort them – and us – to walk by faith so that we may also receive our reward in Eternity.
- To live according to certain specific principles and practise good works.

Most messages I have heard on *Hebrews* were based on chapter 11 and had to do with Faith.

Although this is important, the fact remains that there is much more to it than Faith in this glorious Epistle!

Hebrews is, in fact, a very rich discourse on the superiority and majesty of Jesus, our Heavenly High Priest. It presents Jesus from the vantage point of Heaven in a way that no other Epistle does.

Besides, this spiritual discourse is coupled with practical pieces of advice for a fruitful spiritual walk.

"Therefore let us also, seeing we are surrounded by so great a cloud of witnesses, lay aside every weight and the sin which so easily entangles us, and let us run with patience the race that is set before us, 12:2 looking to Jesus, the author and perfecter of faith, who for the joy that was set before him endured the cross, despising its shame, and has sat down at the right hand of the throne of God."[238]

---

[238] Hebrews 13:1-2.

But, beware: these pieces of advice I call "nuggets" were not meant to be mere "fillers"!

Far from it! They have been given to us to help us in our Christian walk – or better, to help us better run our race!

At the end, each one of us will, then, be able to say like Paul:

"I have fought the good fight. I have finished the course. I have kept the faith. [8] From now on, the crown of righteousness is stored up for me, which the Lord, the righteous judge, will give to me on that day; and not to me

only, but also to all those who have loved his appearing."[239]

Milton Keynes UK
Ingram Content Group UK Ltd.
UKHW021041021124
450589UK00013B/979

9 798227 619655